SINGLE:

not incomplete

ANNIE B. MAYFIELD

Finding fulfillment in a season the world tells you to rush through

SINGLE NOT INCOMPLETE

Published by Happy Self Publishing
www.happyselfpublishing.com
writetous@happyselfpublishing.com

CONTENTS

HEY FRIEND,

If you're reading this right now, I'm assuming it's because your love life is not in its best season. I'll admit that even as I consider myself to be an independent woman, it's hard in a world that worships romantic love to feel confident about your romance-lacking circumstances. When I was little, I grew up watching every Disney adaptation of young love through Lizzie and Gordo on *Lizzie McGuire*, Zoey and Chase on *Zoey 101*, and, of course, Cody and Bailey on *Suite Life on Deck*. Each show left me excited for the moment I'd find "my person." As the years clicked on and I had one relationship end after another, I find myself at 25, feeling a different kind of sentiment when I see young love on screen. Instead of "I can't wait for that!" it turned into "that's not real."

They say you're most qualified to speak to the person you once were. At the beginning of this year, I was in a place of resentment. If I got one more invitation to a wedding that I wouldn't have a date for, or saw one more post from a couple younger than me getting engaged, I was going to burst. This bitterness stemmed from an underlying belief that I was somehow incomplete as a single person. What I realized is that if you're not careful, you can find yourself feeling bitter about a season that God wants to give you as a gift.

As I am writing this, I admit that I still have days where I confuse my worth with my relationship status. When I see cute couples on Instagram, I wonder whether something is wrong with me because I don't have that. In the devotionals to follow, you'll go through the thoughts I had at one time or another during a season of singleness that lasted a lot longer than I anticipated. It's worth noting: I am writing this *still as a single girl*. Most of the books out there on singleness come from those who are now happily married. While there is nothing wrong with that, and their perspective comes with a uniqueness I can't provide, I will say that all this work I've done and shared has been entirely independent of my external circumstances changing. I found my miracle in the changing of my heart and not my relationship status. So, I pray that the transformative potential of the next 40 days encourages you. They go out to each of the girls that I embodied at one time or another in the depths of my insecurity, and it will be coupled with truths from scripture that reframe what would be a destructive thought into a deeper understanding of the opportunity at play. So often we want our healing to be "out there," but the ultimate healing is in our heart. Most women never get to live a life like this. One where she gets to decide how, when, and with whom she spends her time.

Listen, I know it can be hard at times. In the past week, I've had moments where I looked around at all my married or engaged friends and thought, "I'm going to be *that* friend." The one that will have to be a third wheel for the rest of my life. And then? I come back to these truths. I come back to the reminder that the season I am in sets me apart for God to do something unique in me without distraction. What a gift! What a blessing! What a time to live my life, fall in love all over again with *me*, and reconnect deeply with the One that made me before the world labeled me.

Here's to you. Here's to this time. May you be falling in love with yourself every day.

Xoxo,

Annie May

Day 1

THE GIRL WHO'S SEEING EVERYONE ELSE GET MARRIED.

1 Corinthians 7:34: There is also a difference between a wife and a virgin. The unmarried woman careth for the things of the Lord, that she may be holy both in body and in spirit.

I know that sinking feeling. The one where your stomach drops as you continue to get more and more wedding invitations. All the while you keep thinking, "Is it ever going to be me?" In a world that idolizes relationships, it's easy to think you're doing something wrong by not being in one. Not only that you're doing something wrong, but that something is wrong with you. This is the first time I've been single for over a year. While it was exciting at first, the more I grew into this season of my life where everyone is partnering off and getting married, the less confident I became in that status. When I start to confuse my lack of a partner with my worth, I remember what Paul wrote. He reminds us our life purpose *is not to get married*; marriage is an amazing thing to compliment your life's purpose, but the purpose of your life is to glorify God with everything you have. Now I know what you are thinking in the back of your mind. "Gee Annie, that's great! But I'd rather have a cute, fun, hilarious partner to compliment my life's purpose while I glorify God than glorify God alone." And I totally get that. When I have those feelings of jealousy or doubt, I remember that the purpose of marriage is for two people to come together who can better serve the glorification of God in a partnership than by being single. From that, I know that the time in my singleness isn't wasted. God either is strengthening me personally to become ready to receive the partner He has prepared for me, or there are things God is still trying to work through me that I would not have the time or focus for in a partnership. Trust me, I know the gut-punching feeling of *yet another* friend getting engaged. I understand the shame that comes up when the answer to "are you seeing anyone?" is still "nope!" Hear me sister: this time isn't wasted. The fact that we idolize relationships so much is the world's problem, not yours. Don't settle just to join in as another friend in the group who gets her fairytale wedding. You want to be the one who is so excited for the *marriage*; the wedding is a small blip in the story. Use this time. Glorify God in this time. Perhaps one day, as you're running toward Jesus, you'll look to your left and see a *cute* man running that way too.

> **JOT THIS DOWN**
>
> My story isn't theirs. God has already written the best possible story that I could have for the life He gave me, and it is already in motion.

Day 2

THE GIRL WHO THINKS SHE'S TOO BROKEN FOR LOVE.

Psalm 147:3: He heals the brokenhearted and binds up their wounds.

I would like to confess. There's a lot about me that I wish wasn't there. Parts of me I have brushed underneath the surface for too long. How I am constantly trying to please the people who care about me the least, and save my monster-like tendencies for the ones who love me the most. How I can't remember a day in my life when I wasn't thinking about the way my body looked. How I crave to be praised by other people for everything I do. The crippling defeat I feel when I wake up some mornings and my stomach is a little "pudgier," or an injury that stops me from being able to work out all the food I ate the day before. The fear that overwhelms me at night and tells me I'm not good enough. The anxiety in my stomach when I think I am not doing anything with my life. The twitch that comes to my left eye as these thoughts ruminate in my mind. I've pulled myself out of relationships for a long time because of all of the underlying beliefs: "I'm too broken." "No one is ever going to be okay with the rigidness of my routine." "I just wasn't meant to be in a relationship." For years, I've let my worth be spoken through the voice of my brokenness, failing to realize that my brokenness isn't a deviance from love; it is a vessel for it to be carried. In Japanese art there is a technique called *Kintsugi*. Centuries ago, they typically used it for repairing tea sets, and now it's used all over the country for many types of pottery. The only requirement for *Kintsugi*? Broken pottery. You need a bunch of different shards from a glass or a set. After that, the sculptor uses a Japanese lacquer called *urushi* to glue the pieces back together. Writers say that this is the most difficult part of the process because once the *urushi* is dry, nothing can be undone. It can take up to two weeks for the *urushi* to dry, so it is vital that the pot sits in isolation for a time so the repairing can't be sabotaged. After the *urushi* has set into the cracks, the sculptor pours a fine layer of gold, making it a more valuable vessel than its original, crack-less version. Why do I tell you this? When we get our hearts broken, there is a time of uncomfortable healing. Life will hit us so hard through misguided beliefs, expectations, and standards that we break apart; sometimes all at once and sometimes slowly. It's in these moments that we need something sturdy to glue us back together. We need God's love, grace, and mercy. God's love is our *urushi*. With God as the potter, He can pour His love into our broken bits and pull us back together into something even more valuable than before. A partner isn't capable of being your *urushi* but God's love is. This season takes time. It takes time to become whole again when we've been broken for so long. It took time for me to learn to love and speak kindly to my body after 20 years of degrading it. It took time for me to appreciate my discipline after a decade of hiding it from others. It took time for me to practice breathing techniques that would calm my panic attacks. Just as the hardest part of *Kintsugi* is the application and processing, the process of allowing God's love into your brokenness and becoming whole again is difficult. But once it's ready, and you have that firm foundation seeping into your soul and the innermost depths of your insecurities? It's time for the gold. The gold isn't responsible for holding the broken parts together, it simply acts as a gateway for the *urushi* to shine even brighter than it did before. That is the power of what your brokenness can provide. That is the power of waiting to be whole in Christ until He leads you to your gold. Your partner will further emphasize the parts of you that glorify God's goodness. They will deepen the impression of beauty from what was once considered your brokenness to what is now made beautiful through Christ. You may be where I was. Perhaps you have not experienced the *urushi* yet, and you are just sitting with all your broken parts. Or you may be in the waiting period for your *urushi* to dry before your gold is applied. Regardless, know that your brokenness is not a deviance from love. It is the very vein that provides the opportunity to further exemplify God's testimony in your life.

JOT THIS DOWN

My brokenness isn't a deviance from love, but a vessel for it to be carried.

Day 3

THE GIRL WHO'S TOO FOCUSED ON HER CAREER.

Luke 12:6-7: Are not five sparrows sold for two pennies? And not one of them is forgotten before God. Why, even the hairs of your head are all numbered. Fear not; you are of more value than many sparrows.

How I wish I could give you the biggest hug; wrap you in my arms and tell you how beautiful, wonderful, and amazing you are. Not because I feel bad for you, but because I know you. Quite literally, I was you. I've been you. Parts of me still, to this day, correlate with the thoughts I am sure cross your mind fueling your drive. I'm not saying that taking a season to solely focus on hustling is a bad thing. In fact, I think it is an amazing thing. Sprints of "the grind" can be attributed for building some of the most prominent businesses, companies, and empires of our time. However, I am afraid for those who are like me. You looked at having a successful relationship and having a successful career as an either/or. It's impossible to have both. So, like myself, you may have been heartbroken along the way and used your career as a hiding place. I need you to pause for a moment. It was in the moments that I paused that God was able to show me the misaligned definition of "success" that I held. Growing up, the media always portrayed successful women in two capacities. They were an amazing wife/mother, or they had a phenomenal career. Therefore, growing up, I thought my two possible metrics of success were either to be a great family figure or to make a lot of money. I never questioned if there were more metrics of success that I needed to align myself to like health, peace, mindfulness, harmony, energy, radiance, prayer life, divine connection, community, fulfillment, and service. What I failed to recognize growing up was that God gave us our success when He gave us our value. Just as the scripture says, "You are of more value than many sparrows." All along what I was trying to find in these areas of success was my value. Little did I know that my value didn't lay out there. I had a season in my life where my love life was nonexistent and my career was unfulfilling, and I began to enter a dark period. In that time, God was able to finally show me the truth. A relationship and a successful career are not the metrics of value to shoot for. You can have both and still be broken. You can have neither and be the most content version of yourself. So, for my reader who is too focused on her career to have a relationship, I am not asking you to ever (LIKE EVER!) stop that drive. What I am saying is to take a second to recognize why you are driven toward that area so much. Are you running away from the fact that you don't feel worthy of a romantic partnership? Maybe you feel like a failure in the "significant other" department, so you are trying to compensate by becoming extremely successful in your career? Or like me, you bought into the bill of goods that a woman can only be successful in two areas: family or a job, and the family one was too complicated so you went for the career route. Remember that true success isn't confined to those two areas. True success lies in your ability to sit alone in a room stripped of all the things you consider to be your "accolades" (your salary, how big your family is, the size of your house, your awards, etc.) and be perfectly at peace with your Creator. Perhaps when we release ourselves from the need to prove ourselves "out there," we can finally connect to the One who completes us "in here."

JOT THIS DOWN

Work or not. Relationship or not. I am successful because I showed up for this crazy thing called "life" that God blessed me with.

Day 4

THE GIRL WHO THINKS SHE'S LOST THE ONE.

Hebrews 13:5: Never will I leave you; never will I forsake you.

I couldn't even breathe. That is what it felt like when my first college boyfriend of almost a year and a half broke up with me. To capture oxygen in my lungs felt as difficult of a task as finding water in the Sahara. *I just lost the love of my life.* As dramatic as that sounds, for a 19-year-old, that feeling of losing the only person that is ever going to love me in that special way filled my mind. I remember telling my mom time and time again, "I just don't think I'll ever find someone who loves me like that again." Which, honestly, is the truth. Considering every single person is so unique, the way they give love is unique to them. It was and it is still true. I will never again be loved in the way he loved me, but what I failed to realize then was just because I felt I lost "the one and only," doesn't mean I lost my chance for love altogether. When we say we've lost "the one," what we really mean is we lost our chance at ever being loved by that specific person and in that specific way. What that doesn't mean is that we lost our chance at being loved all together. There was an 87-year-old woman who lost her husband when he fell off a roof trying to make a repair. After 2 years of sitting in bed and suffering from depression, she felt the Lord say, "Agnus you may have lost your husband, but you didn't lose the love of your life. *I* am the love of your life." When we think of God's love for us in that way, every single relationship we get the chance to experience is simply a borrowed gift of time. You cannot lose something you never truly had ownership of. Even the man you spent your entire life with eventually passes away; you never owned him. He was a gift. His love was a gift. A gift that the love of your life gave you. If you're anything like me, you will have multiple instances where you think you've lost the one. The one that holds the key to your heart. The one that loves you enough to put up with all your brokenness. The one that knows what you're going to say before you even say it. The one you've dreamed of building a family with. The first one you want to call when something amazing has happened because you know that your win is their win too. The one you immediately want to cry to when everything falls apart. There are a lot of those "ones" because each person you open your heart to is going to love you in such a deep and unique way (romantically or platonically). When we remember that every great love that comes into our life is meant to be a further expression of the One who is love itself, we can then appreciate each of them for the season God needed them to be there. My beautiful girl, you didn't lose "the one." It isn't possible. Not the *true* one. Because He who is the true one will never leave you and never forsake you (Hebrew 13:5).

JOT THIS DOWN

The right person at the wrong time is still the wrong person. The wrong person at the right time is still the wrong person.

Day 5

THE GIRL WHO DOESN'T KNOW HOW TO LET SOMEONE LOVE HER.

1 John 4:18: There is no fear in love; but perfect love casts out fear because fear has torment.

"Protecting myself." That's what I've always called it. AKA hiding myself from anyone looking close enough at me to be disappointed with what they saw. Looking back at my life, I had told three individuals that I have fallen in love with them. I heard from each of them in return. When I really think about it though, I'm not quite sure if these people fell in love with *me* or the *me* I created to gain their approval. I've always been able to read a crowd. I can easily morph myself into exactly the person I think you need me to be. Funny, witty, charming, outgoing, quiet, skinny, curvy, smart, dumbed-down, action-taker, or reserved? Take your pick, I can do it all. On that quest to be who I think the person I am with needs me to be in order to feel good about themselves, I buried the real parts of myself. The one that didn't know what she was doing. The one that didn't have a plan. The one that falls prey to her ego and greed. The one that isn't happy all the time. I hid because I was certain if the person I loved saw the real me, they would flee. So, I put on a mask that I was certain they would love. Honestly? All that did was leave me feeling empty. In trying to protect myself from getting hurt, I was hurting myself. "How do I make them love me?" That was the question I thought I was trying to answer this entire time, but what I was really trying to answer was: *How can I shapeshift myself enough to ensure someone never hurts me?* The truth, whether it is manufactured or the real deal, love doesn't come without hurt. There is no guarantee you won't be left, forgotten, or rejected. What I can guarantee you is that the pain of someone loving the you that you've curated to match their needs is far heavier than the pain of someone rejecting the real you. I can't say you're protected from experiencing pain when you show up as the real, broken, and raw you, but I can promise you will go through a far worse pain if you show up as only a made-up, polished, and glossed over version to prevent them from leaving. Love between two people wasn't designed to be perfect, just honest. God is the only One capable of perfect love. Honest love is what we are all after. Honest love between our family, friends, and significant others. Honest love is a love that isn't based in fear. Because He knows everything in our hearts, there is no room for hiding. Where there is light and truth, no fear can be present. So, how do you let someone love you? It starts with one step: letting someone see the real you so no fear can blossom in the gaps you've been trying to cover.

JOT THIS DOWN

Love doesn't have to be perfect; it has to be honest.

Day 6

THE GIRL WHO FORGOT WHAT IT FELT LIKE TO BE LOVED.

John 1:3: Through him all things were made, and apart from him nothing was made that has been. He created everything there is—nothing exists that he didn't make.

Our skin cells begin to replace themselves every 14–50 days (depending on our age). When I was younger and fell into my first heartbreak, I remember finding comfort in this. Thinking that in just 14 days, my body will already be turning into a body that he never hugged. That the skin around my hand will soon be that which he never held. The skin on my lips will eventually be skin he never kissed. Basically, what I believed was that at some point in the proceeding 14–50 days, the version of myself that was associated with him would cease to exist. While I didn't account for my internal wounds having to go through a much slower process than my skin, I did find that after a while I forgot what it was like to have someone be in love with you. Not just the physical aspects but the little parts of a relationship that provide comfort. The good night and good morning texts. Someone who may ask, "How is your day going?" A go-to person to vent to, random facetimes in the middle of the day, someone to cry and laugh with, or a person who is just, if not more, excited about your success than you are. It all becomes a blur with enough time. Maybe you've been there too. It has been so long since you've opened yourself up to someone that you forgot what it was like to be in love. For some of you this is reassuring because you're in the thick of hurting right now and the idea of "forgetting" what love feels like would be an answered prayer if it also meant taking away the pain you feel from its loss. However, for those whose wounds are now scars and the aching of heartbreak is long gone, it's easy to associate the lack of romantic love within our lives, as a lack of capacity for us to hold it. In psychology, there is a type of conditioning called operant conditioning. This is where rewards are given when the subject does something correctly, and punishment is given when done incorrectly. In our world, we are conditioned to believe that being loved by someone is a reward we get for being "enough" and not being loved by someone is a punishment for "not being enough." For people who aren't receiving the "reward" of being loved by someone, they can begin to take that as an indication that they are doing something wrong. Their punishment is a lack of romantic love in their life and somehow they are unlovable. Have you been there? I've been there more times than I can count. It's been almost two years since I've really let anyone in. I can barely remember what it feels like to be in love. When I was younger, these pauses in my relationship status left me feeling inadequate and insecure. What I've begun to realize through time is that we tend to miss the marks of the greatest love all around us every day. We look for hand holds, hugs, kisses, words of affirmation, and cute messages from partners as affirmation of our ability to be loved. What if we are receiving that every day from the One who's made in the image of love without even realizing it? John 1:3 tells us that God made everything in the world. That building you see outside? He made the materials that made that building. The mountain you see in the distance? He made that too. Rain falling down, technology, science, people: all of it was made by Him. What if every single day when the wind touches your face, it is God reminding you that He is there. What if each time the rain falls from the sky and splatters against your coat, it serves as an indication that

He is pouring His love on you. What if every tree, glint of sunshine, animal skipping across the road, and cloud in the sky could remind you that love encompasses you everywhere. The One who is love, loves you so much, and every day He sends signals of that love to you. Once I realized that, the irony is that even in what is my longest gap from being in a relationship, I have never felt more loved. Why? Because I am touched everyday by the love of my Creator. He has everlasting love for me every single second.

JOT THIS DOWN

Love is a state of connection with the One who created love, not a status to achieve by means of another person.

THE GIRL WHO IS A SERIAL DATER.

John 14:27: Peace I leave with you; my peace I give you. I do not give to you as the world gives. Do not let your hearts be troubled and do not be afraid.

Boy #1 broke my heart. I immediately wanted to find boy #2. Boy #2 wasn't a "significant" relationship, but it did the job of distracting me from my heartbreak of boy #1. Boy #3 was a *real* relationship. Helped me officially get over boy #1. Boy #3 didn't work out. I almost instantly found boy #4. After boy #4 and I thought we'd spend the rest of our lives together but ended up calling it quits. I was too tired to find boy #5. For the first time in my life, I wasn't looking to outsource my healing. My broken heart was patiently waiting for "time" to assume the role of a healer and not another relationship. Truthfully? I didn't think "time" would work. Almost like an experiment I was opting into, I wanted to see if time really did heal all wounds. Up until that point I was convinced the only way to get over someone is to move on to another relationship, so you can distract yourself from thinking about the former. While I do think it's important we surround ourselves with the right people when we are going through a healing season, I've come to realize all of those years I spent running from one guy to the next led me to project insecurities onto them that they never had a hand in creating. Refusing to heal your cuts will cause you to bleed on people that didn't cut you. All this time I thought that finding the next guy was going to make me heal faster, but all it did was create further distance between my awareness and the underlying wounds I was running from. I didn't know it was possible to experience healing in such a way where you don't have to run to another version of the situation that broke your heart in the first place. I was watching the Matthew Perry documentary the other day. He said that the first time he experienced drugs, he fell in love with them because they made him feel like he didn't need alcohol. He was so appreciative to have a break from the constant torment of needing alcohol, but his new refuge led to another imprisonment. We do this a lot in relationships. We become obsessed with the idea of the next guy because it gives us temporary relief from the heartbreak of the last. But all that is going to do is bring you right back into the cycle of the pain you ran away from. Getting into a relationship because together you both do greater good for the Gospel and getting into a relationship to serve as a crutch from your current brokenness are two very different things. Have the courage to do the work. Take time for your heart to heal. Honor yourself with the gift of reflection. The intention behind diving into the next relationship is everything. It rarely has anything to do with time. You may, in fact, find the love of your life 2 weeks after a breakup, and that's amazing. For some, it may take 2 years. Regardless, it is the intention I want you to look at. Why are you going into this relationship? Why are you choosing to partner with this man? Are you partnering with him to run together toward Christ or to run away from the pain you feel in your heart that you don't want to deal with? The world will tell you to run all day from what is bothering you; numb it with social media, food, drinking, partying, sleeping, or work. God reminds us that He does not give us peace as the world gives us peace. We aren't going to find peace by striving for our next relationship status. It is going to come from a place deeper within, but we must first slow ourselves down to receive it.

> **JOT THIS DOWN**
>
> **It is a brave thing to choose the painful path of honest healing, rather than the easy path of romantic distraction.**

Day 8

THE GIRL WHO IS DATING A DUD.

Proverbs 27:17: Iron sharpens iron, and one man sharpens another.

Too scared to let go. That is typically the feeling I have when I am in a situation that I'm not necessarily content to be in, but the fear of stepping into the unknown is greater. There's been moments in my life, typically toward the end of the three significant relationships I've held, when I knew in my gut that the person I was with wasn't my person, and I wasn't theirs either. Although my heart knew, my head would start calculating all the reasons why letting them go was too risky. I'd think of how much I liked their family, how much their family liked me, the upcoming plans we'd made, the history we've established, or how nice it was to automatically have someone for every event where a partner was needed. According to the calculations in my brain, being "potentially happier" wasn't reason enough to leave the comfort zone I had created. That being said, no matter how hard I tried there was still that small voice in my heart that not even my comfort zone could silence. Every time I've talked to someone in a relationship who can't seem to let go, it's always because even though they know there may be more out there, they aren't willing to let go of the comfortable. I'll be the first to say, letting go of a "fine" relationship that is incredibly comfortable for the possibility of a better one that doesn't exist yet is incredibly hard. However, what I know to be true is the long-term pain of staying in a "fine" and familiar relationship will always be greater than the pain of leaving for the potential of a more fulfilling life. I didn't say a more fulfilling *relationship* because I don't think God gives us nudges to take on a greater trajectory for our life for the mere purpose of a partnership with another person. I think He puts little hints in our hearts when it's time to go, so that we can step into a deeper part of our relationship with Him. Whether that includes an amazing partner or not can only be determined when we take that step toward the place He is calling us to. I'm not sure our society realizes just how important the person you choose to spend the rest of your life with is. As Proverbs mentions, "Iron sharpens iron." That doesn't mean it is always supposed to feel good when you are with the right company, but that the right company will be the type of people that make you better. Their insight, faith, love, kindness, and care will make you want to be a better version of yourself regardless of how painful it may be for you to level up in those areas. Just as that is true, the contrary is true too. If you are with someone who doesn't challenge you to become a better version of yourself, you are going to start regressing in the progress made. In life, you are either growing or shrinking. There is no neutral. That is why it is so important to have high standards for who you are choosing to do life with. It is better to be alone than to be with stagnant company. That person influences you more than any other person on the planet. Your mom, dad, sister, brother, coworkers, or best friends do not influence you like your partner does. If that relationship you are experiencing isn't bringing you closer to the Father, I would offer the perspective that it is a more dangerous decision to stay. Being single is painful at first but staying with a guy that isn't treating you right or isn't the one you know God meant to have you run alongside as you grow in faith is more painful. So, how painful will it be? When I asked myself this question, I looked at the outcomes. To choose to stay in that very "fine" relationship would lead to a very "fine" outcome. To choose to part ways lovingly but with the intention to answer that nudge in my Spirit to move in the next direction would result in my ultimate growth. For me, the outcome of ultimate growth was enough of a light to get me through the dark tunnel when first making that decision. Now that I am on the other side, I want to tell you, my beautiful friend, who may be dating a dud because you're afraid of being alone: the tunnel that follows the choice to step out on the nudge from your Spirit is darker yet shorter than the never-ending tunnel that results from choosing to stay in a place that isn't helping you grow.

JOT THIS DOWN

The uncomfortable decision to move forward on what the Spirit is nudging me to do is better than any default decision to remain in my comfort zone.

THE GIRL WHO HAS BAGGAGE.

John 20:27: Put your finger here, and see my hands; and put out your hand, and place it on my side. Do not disbelieve, but believe.

I have kissed a total of seven boys in my life. I was in a serious relationship with three of them. The other four consisted of music festival venues and poor judgment. That being said, each time I kissed someone, whether it was a significant partner or not, I had this realization that one day they would be part of the story I would tell my someone special. You know that whole process where you begin dating someone seriously and all of a sudden it is time for "the conversation" where you open up about your past or "baggage" as my friends in high school liked to call it. I remember one friend in particular who would say, "your baggage just got a bit heavier" every time one of us would make a stupid decision with a guy or kiss someone unexpectedly. What a nice comment to receive. We live in a world that is quick to promote all the things that lead us to gathering more baggage but is also quick to judge when we add any baggage to our load. Our music, movies, and media is all governed around sex, lust, and bodies, but no one wants to deal with the raw pain underneath all the wounds that come from constantly giving into temptations. Baggage has become a derogatory term. We all want to participate in the things that the world celebrates, but no one wants to carry the baggage that comes from it. So, what do we do? We hide it all. Like our dirty laundry all over the dorm room, we shove it under the bed when our crush decides to come hang. It's out of sight, but never was dealt with. Messes unattended start to stink. Baggage never unloaded begins to get heavier. Overtime, our baggage starts piling up so much that we tell ourselves it's too heavy to open up to anyone about. That, or, if you have opened up to someone in the past, and it didn't work out, you tell yourself the story that you can't ever make yourself that vulnerable again. I felt this way before. The first guy I dated seriously in college is one who I opened myself up to in ways I hadn't in the past. I was honest about the jealousy I'd feel at times. I told him about my struggles with body image. The secrets about my fear of never being good enough were exposed. When that relationship didn't work out, I felt the safest thing to do was to never open myself up like that again. To show someone my scars like that meant giving them a weapon they could use against me, and that wasn't safe. It wasn't until I got into my next relationship, and slowly but surely began to open up to him, that I realized scars can be the bridgeway to connection with the right person. Jesus shows us the revealing of your scars can bring people back to the One who heals them all. Jesus didn't come back without a trace of what happened to Him on the cross. He came with scars to tell the story, but in that portrayal of those scars, He served as a testimony for the One who got Him through it. When we share our scars with the right people, not only does it make way for a deeper connection but it brings people back to the One who got you through the thing that created the scar in the first place. If you are living this human existence, you are going to have scars, baggage, and pain. It will get heavy at times. It will get lonely at times. There will be times when the scars you thought had fully healed, start stinging again. There will be people in this life, *special* people, who you can show your scars to. It will bring both of you back to the One who led you to overcome the source of the scar. Baggage isn't a bad thing; it tells your story. Scars aren't a bad thing; they are reminders of the One who led your raw wound to heal. Scars aren't meant to be shown to everyone, but they are meant to be shared with the special people that God is urging you to bridge a connection with. You can't have too many scars that disqualify you from connection. I promise. Jesus showed His scars, so why would we be ashamed to show ours? The more baggage you have, the more details of your story that can be used to deepen a connection with someone as you progress in your relationship journey.

JOT THIS DOWN

I deserve a love that loves *all* of me, not the parts of me that don't have scars.

Day 10

THE GIRL WHO FEELS THE NEED TO EXPLAIN HERSELF.

Proverbs 18:21: The tongue has the power of life and death, and those who love it will eat its fruit.

Three words. *Holiday. Work. Parties.* Honestly, I wouldn't mind them much if it wasn't for the "plus one" that followed every invitation. And, no, it isn't that I don't know how to have fun by myself. In fact, I find no greater delight in going to a party where I know I can leave whenever I want because I'm only looking out for a party of one. However, there is the constant "Oh, you're not seeing anyone?" "Oh, where's your plus one?" "Oh, I think I have a friend that you'd love!" "Oh, don't worry sweetie; I was single for years before I met *introduces me to the one she met after all those miserable solo years right then and there*."* As if being single is some crazy disease that I am just sitting with and begging for the people around me to cure by introducing me to all their friends. I'll be honest. Every time someone asks me about my relationship status, I always feel the need to explain its absence in my life. Like two conjunctions forever glued together with a comma. When someone asks if I am single, it is always, "Yes I am single right now, **but** I was in a long relationship previously. It didn't work out so I've just been taking a break." For many of us, being single is a layup for the run-on sentence filled with explanations as to why we found ourselves this way. All to imply that our singleness isn't strong enough to stand on its own without explanation; that we wouldn't choose to be this way if it wasn't for *insert our explanation here*. Anyone else sick of the main metric of success for a woman predicated on her relationship status? Someone once told me that "no" is not a run-on sentence. I wonder if "Yes, I am single" can also refrain from being a run-on sentence. If it is true that we tend to explain away the things we feel shame about, perhaps we need to start asking why we feel so much shame around our singleness? To be a woman capable of providing for herself, taking care of her body, loving herself, and finding a love so deeply rooted in her Creator that she isn't necessarily looking for external vices through men. When broken down like that I have no idea why I feel the need to explain my singleness. Scripture teaches us that the power of life and death lies in the tongue. If this is so, how we speak about this season of our lives dictates the energy that follows suit. Every time I fall prey to my conditioning of explaining away what could be the most foundational season of my life, I belittle its significance. I am telling myself the story that I am someone whose circumstances need an explanation because they aren't strong enough to stand just as they are. Like a face caked with makeup, we feel the need to hide what's going on underneath even though that is where the real beauty lies. Just as your beautiful face doesn't need covering, neither does your current story. Your singleness isn't a run-on sentence. There is power in the tongue and, sometimes, refraining from further explanation is the most powerful explanation to give.

JOT THIS DOWN

There is no shame around what could be one of the most pivotal seasons of my life.

Day 11

THE GIRL WHO HAS CONFUSED 'BEING ALONE' WITH LONELINESS.

Mark 1:35: And in the early morning, while it was still dark, Jesus got up, left the house, and went away to a secluded place, and prayed there for a time.

I can remember the first time I realized that I loved to be alone. It was on the Morris Brandon playground behind the large hedges where there was enough room for a little girl to play with sticks in the sand before the cement walls crept in. All day I couldn't wait to get to my spot behind the bushes. Did I do this every time? No. There were times Louise or Margaret would ask me to play, and I would. But honestly, each time I did, I missed my little spot behind the bushes. Even as a little kid I never had trouble being alone. In fact, I looked forward to it.

It was the only time I felt like I could actually tap into what I was thinking. All day teachers told me what to think, coaches told me how to practice, and friends chimed in on how I should act. When I was just with myself, there were no expectations; I could just be. There are two interpretations behind the act of being alone: loneliness and solitude. We live in a world that has by default accepted the nature of being alone with loneliness. If you are all by yourself there must be something wrong with you. In fact, we are so averse to just being by ourselves that if we go for a meal by ourselves, we are constantly on our phone. As if to say, "I promise I have other things to watch or people to talk to. I am not alone in life even though I am alone here." But what's so bad about it? Jesus spent decades alone before His ministry started at 33. He sought out alone time each morning. So why are we so averse to being alone? I think it's because we aren't looking at the second option—solitude. As a little girl behind the hedges, I didn't feel alone even when I was all by myself. I felt I was in solitude. To be in solitude takes a strong stance around being all by yourself. Being single doesn't mean you are alone. This could possibly be the first chance for you to actually tune into what your Spirit is calling you toward. Just as Jesus sought to be alone each morning, so He can speak with the Father. Being by oneself is a good thing to yearn for. It's not only a good thing to search for in your day-to-day routine, or for seasons at a time, but it is also completely necessary no matter what stage of life you are in. This is a special time to connect with yourself more deeply than you may ever get to again. Once Jesus's ministry took off, He wasn't able to spend the expanse of time alone He had prior because He became known by all. The same goes for the foundation of awareness that can be the fruit that comes from this season of singleness. You will be able to use the good that comes from this time for years and with any path that comes your way.

JOT THIS DOWN

I may never get the chance to be this in tune with myself again.

Day 12

THE GIRL WHO FEELS SHAME AROUND HER SINGLE STRUGGLE.

Philippians 1:6: God is the one who began this good work in you, and I am certain that he won't stop before it is complete on the day that Christ Jesus returns.

Growing up, I always had a hard time telling people when I was hurting. There was something in my bones that associated pain as weakness. I felt that a "good girl" was one that didn't feel sadness or pain. To be the perfect kid, I had to also have the perfect personality, looks, grades, friendships, and boyfriend. Feeling sad didn't fit into my criteria of perfection, which forced me to constantly numb pain. Whether it is someone talking about me behind my back, the zit on my nose, how I hated the way my stomach looked in a bikini, or the fear that no guy was really going to like me for *me*, I felt shame around any struggle. Now, as a single woman for almost 2 years, the shame of my singleness creeps in no matter how hard I try to shove it down. For a while being single was a relief. After moving from one relationship to the next, it felt like a breath of fresh air to carry my own for once. Not having to respond to anyone, let them know where I was, wait for them to get home to send a good night text before I went to bed; it felt amazing. However, it was the very things I was so relieved to not have anymore, I found myself missing the most. Now that it's been so long that I've been single, I don't have much of an explanation as to why. Before I could say I just got out of a relationship, but now there is no reason when people ask about whether I am seeing anyone or not. The gaps where I believe my explanation should lay are where shame creeps in. I know I'm not alone in the dating struggle, and I fear that so many of us accept our struggle as an indication that we aren't worthy of the thing we are struggling for. We tell ourselves the "victory of a relationship" just isn't in the cards for us. What I want to remind you is that your struggle isn't an indication you're losing the fight, but an indication that you're alive to fight the battle. In war, there are two types of soldiers. Those that have a serene expression in battle, and those that are on edge as they struggle to continue to fight. The soldiers that are still and serene? They are the ones who are no longer alive to fight the battle. All living soldiers fighting a battle having struggle written all over their face. To struggle isn't a bad thing and doesn't make you any less worthy of the thing you are fighting for. In fact, it is living proof that you are still here by the grace of God to go after the thing in your heart. If you still struggle with being single, that means God has put a relationship in your heart. He who began that design in you to yearn for a relationship will be faithful to complete it but on His timeline. This struggle season that He has you in now forges you into the person He needs you to become to receive the goodness of the relationship He has planned. Your struggle means you're still here. Still alive. Still able to fight the fight toward the thing God put in your heart. Realize that not everyone struggles with being single. The fact that you are struggling means God gave that hope to you. He designed your heart to crave a relationship, and that is a good thing. Struggling for it doesn't mean you aren't going to get it or are in the process of attaining it wrong. It means you are in the middle of what will one day be the tale of how God created you into the person mature enough to receive the one coming. Do not be ashamed of the struggle; it is the promise of the victory to come.

> **JOT THIS DOWN**
>
> **My struggle is an indication that I'm still in the fight for victory of how God has designed my heart.**

Day 13

THE GIRL WHO DOESN'T KNOW HOW TO DATE.

---

1 John 4:7: Dear friends, let us love one another, for love comes from God. Everyone who loves has been born of God and knows God. Whoever does not love does not know God, because God is love.

I am 25, and I have no idea how to date in today's world. My past three serious relationships were matches found in school. No one told me that after you graduated it became incredibly (quite impossible) hard to meet someone out in the wild. On top of that, I am literally an 85-year-old at heart. This makes my preference to stay in very compelling, and you understand why my sister had to sit me down and tell me that even though it is unfair, great guys don't just fall from your living room ceiling. I hadn't noticed how disconnected I was from the dating scene until I recently decided to be on it. It's like tennis. You don't know how bad you are at tennis until you go and try to play for yourself. Looking at a professional on TV you think, "I've got this in the bag; how hard can it be?" Until you are brutally humbled by the fact that even though it looks easy, it's incredibly tedious; very similar to today's dating scene I mean. Do you download the app or do you not? Do you initiate or let the guy? What does a "date" even look like nowadays? For followers of Christ, I think it's important to understand that while the Bible doesn't talk much about dating, it does talk a lot about evaluation. Learning how to date should come from the One who created love in the first place. Ben Stuart says, "Dating is not a status you sit in; it is a process you move through." Our world has turned dating into a cul-de-sac where relationships go to sit. The intention of dating is everything. I have no idea how to "date" in 2023's world. I do know that as a follower of Christ, linking arms with another follower of Christ follower is important. I do know that intention, clarity, and trust is important. My ladies, if the guy isn't clear on what he wants to do then he isn't clear on how he feels about you. Otherwise, he isn't mature enough to respect your time and energy. Dating should be clear. It should have momentum. It is the filtering of a process designed to get to that next step in a relationship. John tells us that God is love. To search for love in a dating relationship means to rest it on the cornerstone of Him. It's okay if you don't know the ins and outs of how to date and do all the things just as it is okay to show up to your first tennis lesson not knowing the details of every stroke or shot. What's most important is knowing your intention for being out there. Who do you hope to link arms with as your partner? What kind of person are you looking for? It's hard to put yourself on court when you aren't clear about the ideal outcome of the match.

JOT THIS DOWN

You don't need to know "how to date." You just need to be following Christ, and your Spirit will guide you through the rest.

Day 14

THE GIRL PISSED OFF ABOUT HER SINGLENESS.

James 1:17: Every good and perfect gift is from above, coming down from the Father of the heavenly lights, who does not change like shifting shadows.

"Pissed!" I bet you didn't think you'd see that word in a devotional book, did you? I sometimes feel like we forget God is God, which means He's strong enough to handle how we really feel. To some, "pissed off" about a season of singleness is incredibly confusing, but for others, that is your exact sentiment. At first, it doesn't start as anger; it starts as irritation. Maybe you just got out of a relationship or have been in a bit of a dry season for a while. Not having met anyone you're remotely curious to put a cute outfit on for instead of your sweatpants, and it doesn't bother you too much until Sally suddenly meets the love of her life. She hasn't been out of a relationship for the duration of a sneeze, and all of a sudden she's met some charming new prince. Then your friend, Lauren, who doesn't even go to church meets a guy that is sweet, patient, kind, and loving. That's when you start looking at God with surprise. All these prayers you've been praying in church, and they get the thing you've been wanting for so long? The tipping point is when your friend Ashley facetimes you after meeting a guy on Hinge three months ago. You can feel in your gut what's coming: "We're engaged!" Irritation turns to frustration and then to anger, which turns to "I'm pissed off." Don't you love the fact that God can handle your real emotions? That'll free some of you right there. Just knowing that you can pray to God in the way you really are feeling. And guess what? He already knows all those thoughts running through your head. Someone told me the other day that green lights are only as effective as red lights. Think about it. If every single traffic light on the road was green, there would be mass chaos everywhere you turn. People would be running into each other, crashing their cars, speeding, slowing down too much, and it wouldn't be safe. Are red lights annoying? Absolutely. Do they take a long time? Sure. But are they necessary? Yes. You're still going to reach where you're going, but we need the red lights to prevent harm from coming our way as we journey to get there. My beautiful friend, I know this season is one where you feel God has given you a big, fat red light in your life. This stagnant dating terminal feels like it's jeopardizing your desired marriage destination, but I promise it isn't. The green lights are only as effective as the red lights. God gives us the gift of red lights, so that we are protected from harm. We don't even know what would come our way if He only gave us green lights to everything we wanted in life. It's okay to be angry, but don't lose faith. James tells us that every good and perfect thing comes from the Lord. This includes the moments He tells us no. This red-light season is serving a deeper service of protection, patience, character-building, and order that goes beyond our understanding. This red light doesn't prevent you from getting to your destination; it is there to safely transport you along the way.

JOT THIS DOWN

God says "no" not because He hates us, but because He is protecting us.

Day 15

THE GIRL WHO DOESN'T WANT TO WANT IT ANYMORE.

Psalm 34:10: Even strong young lions sometimes go hungry, but those who trust in the Lord will lack no good thing.

During my freshman year at college, I didn't make the starting line-up for the tennis team. I was beyond crushed. I had been working my butt off for the past 2 years to have a chance and start in the top 6, but I wasn't good enough for it. I remember the match of the season where it really sunk in. We were playing at home, and everyone came to watch. People were coming up to me asking when I was going to be playing, and it killed me to respond that I wasn't because I didn't make the top 6. I was embarrassed, ashamed, and felt like everything I had done until that point was a waste. As more and more matches went on where I kept the benches warm, the frustration began to pile up. Not because I wasn't playing. I had made peace with that. However, the desire to want to play continued to keep me up at night. It was extremely evident that I wasn't going to have a shot this season, but the adrenaline pumping in my veins, thirsty for a chance to go in, wouldn't stop. After a while, my prayers changed from "God, can you make a way for me to get in the line-up" to "God, can you take this desire out of my heart to want to be in the line-up." Sometimes you get to a point where the lack of the thing you want in your life isn't what's hurting you most; it's the longing in your heart. You feel as if you're setting yourself up for failure because you want something you're never going to have. I got to that point with relationships. Driving back from another dud of a date (nothing against the guy I went out with, but there was just no spark), I asked God to take this desire to want a significant other from my heart if it's not in His plans for me. I didn't want to want it anymore. All of a sudden, my hunger for this thing that apparently may not happen was a burden that I wanted gone. Not having something the world wants isn't a problem if you don't personally want it. To not be hungry for something the world is starving for isn't a problem if you aren't personally starving for it. The Psalmist tells us that "Even strong, young lions sometimes go hungry, but those who trust in the Lord will lack no good thing." (Psalm 34:10). When I read that this morning, it hit home. It reminded me that being hungry for something doesn't mean you're lacking something. To have a hunger in your heart, if anything, is an indication from God that there is something to feed you out there. The problem is when we look in the wrong places. The lions may be hungry, but they don't lack. You may be hungry for that significant other, but in the midst of that hunger, it doesn't mean your life is lacking anything. During the course of desiring a partner, you are still completely whole in Christ. To want is not to lack. Anxiety starts to creep into our minds when we associate our longing for a lack. Remind yourself that you are not lacking even in your wanting, hunger, and desire. When you realize that, you're able to want from a place of hope and not a place of deficiency. That is when the process of longing becomes enjoyable and not a burden.

JOT THIS DOWN

You may be hungry for that significant other, but in the midst of that hunger it doesn't mean your life is lacking anything.

Day 16

THE GIRL WHO THINKS GOD IS SMALLER THAN HER PROBLEMS.

Ecclesiastes 9:1: For all this I considered in my heart even to declare all this, that the righteous, and the wise, and their works, are in the hand of God: no man knoweth either love or hatred by all that is before them.

When I was younger, I used to think that when it rained outside, the raindrops were God's tears falling down on this world. In the back of my mom's Toyota Sequoia, I would stare out the window at all the drops coming down and think, "What did I do wrong that made you cry, God?" My mind would wander back to all the things I did that day. Maybe it was because someone stole our teacher's dry erase marker and hid it. That made God so sad! Or maybe it was because Lelia fell during the jump rope and everyone laughed at her. That's why He is so sad! Growing up, without realizing it, I looked at any problem in my life as a challenge for God;

something that He couldn't handle. Sounds silly when we're talking about dry erase markers and failed jump rope routines, but don't we still do that in our everyday lives? Sure, as we get older our problems become more pressing and a bit deeper, but every time something goes wrong, part of our heartache, whether we realize it or not, stems from this underlying belief that we aren't so sure if God can handle what just happened. My brother was in a car accident last week, and the news almost killed me. I can remember not breathing when my sister called me because the thought of losing him was enough to stop my lungs from processing air. Previously, I thought that having a partner was a necessity when going through things like this. I'd never suffered the loss or potential loss of a loved one as a single person. Honestly, I wasn't sure if I could handle it. When I questioned whether or not I was capable of handling it, I was inadvertently questioning if God could handle it too. If it is true that He is the source of our strength, when we think we aren't going to get through something, we are questioning His capabilities and not just ours. My brother getting into that accident wasn't the first painful moment I've had since being single, and it won't be the last. But you know the amazing thing God has taught me through the process? He is big enough for it all. Every single, little thing. I would've never truly known that had I not gone through a few hardships when I didn't have my prince charming to run to. This is not to say that you don't need community when going through hard times, but there is a difference in running to additional help knowing God has your back and running to people because you fear He doesn't. God really is stronger than the battle you are facing. I promise. I *pinkie* promise. Perhaps the bigger the problems we face, the bigger revelations God is using to introduce us to the different capacities of Him, so we can continue to know He isn't the God of our limitations. His scope, breadth, power, and ability span further than we will ever comprehend here on this Earth. Each piece of adversity we face is another crack in the doorway as we peek unto His magnitude. Know that all things, people, and instances go through His hands. Whatever you are going through, and even though you may be fighting that battle as a single person, you aren't fighting alone. God is bigger than what you are facing. I promise.

JOT THIS DOWN

God doesn't shrink to the level of the limitations we put on Him.

THE GIRL WHO WANTS HER PARTNER TO BE EQUALLY YOKED.

2 Corinthians 6:14: Do not be unequally yoked with unbelievers. For what partnership has righteousness with lawlessness? Or what fellowship has light with darkness?

The past three relationships that I've had, have all been fine. Truly. I am fortunate to say there was no abuse, manipulation, or, for the most part, toxicity. The breaking of each had more to do with timing than anything else. Even then, there was always this nagging in my heart within those relationships. A nagging that, at the time, I couldn't articulate. However, now that I've had the gift of hindsight, I recognize that this internal nagging was around this idea of being in an equally yoked partnership. What the heck does that mean? It has to do with one's ability to help carry the weight of something toward a destination. This comes to us from the Bible in a farming context where oxen are yoked together to help carry the cart behind them. In America, we know little about this because we replaced horses with oxen, which were then replaced with tractors. What's interesting about oxen is that one ox alone can pull an amount equal to or greater than their body weight, which is around 1500–3000 lbs. However, when you pair it with another ox, they not only pull more (over 6000 lbs.), but it makes the load easier on the two to carry. In current day American culture, we see marriage and relationships as two people living separate lives but coming together for certain things. Each of them are separate individuals carrying their own cart behind them. What God intended was for us to be paired with another so that our load feels lighter. To partner up with another team member, so not only can we handle more as we navigate the fields of life, but also let that companionship allow our experience to be smoother. The biggest problem farmers will tell you when a load isn't carried successfully is that one of the oxen wasn't equally yoked with the other. One of them may have been smaller or not as strong, so the weight wasn't dispersed evenly. Thus, what was designed to be a process of increasing ease turned into something that created more difficulty. Now I'm not saying you need to find someone in life that matches with you on the things that the world celebrates: looks, fitness, and finances, but a love for

God is key. That is what the nagging was in my heart all those years ago within each of those relationships. It's why I felt so hesitant to bind my life with the other. To be equally yoked is incredibly important, but also remember that your love for God is going to look different than someone else's love for God. This is something I have to remind myself because I used to think equally yoked meant having someone whose relationship with God is just like mine, but that isn't the case. Just as all hearts are different, everyone's relationship with God is going to look different. So how do you know if you are equally yoked? Look at who owns their heart. Be very weary, my friend, of giving your heart to a man that hasn't first given his to God. It is a lofty thing to have a man love you more than he loves God. That is a weight you will never be able to hold without crumbling. Whoever you end up with needs God. They must know just how much they need God in order to partner with you on the fields of life as we carry the weight of our baggage on our way to the promised land.

JOT THIS DOWN

Before you give your heart to a man, make sure he has given it to God.

Day 18

THE GIRL THAT NEEDS A LOVE DETOX.

1 Corinthians 13:4–8: Love is patient and kind; love does not envy or boast; it is not arrogant or rude. It does not insist on its own way; it is not irritable or resentful; it does not rejoice at wrongdoing, but rejoices with the truth.

I fast every Monday. Now, I know fasting has become a trendy word of sorts, so let me clarify what I do when I fast. This is basically a 24-hour period when I only drink water and black coffee. I used to hate Mondays because of this very reason. I woke up feeling bleh knowing that it was a day I couldn't look forward to a rice cake with peanut butter or a smoothie topped with a pinch of cinnamon. And yes, I still have those moments when I want the day to just go by as soon as possible. I have been doing this for the past four years. I now realize that the benefit of giving my body a reset isn't really experienced until days after I've done it. Throughout the week, it's like my appetite has been reset. I don't crave the sugary candy like I used to. The smell of fries or donuts are no longer a weak point for me. Heck, I don't even dream about bread! Before I got into this practice, I would feel hungry almost all the time. I thought I needed way more food than my body actually did. I craved almost everything and would snack nonstop between meals. Giving my body a brief break at the beginning of the week resets my digestion system to regulate its normal functioning. I think some of us need to do that with our hearts. We've been told by this world what love looks like. That love is a crazy, chaotic, emotional roller coaster that requires codependency, but that was never the initial design for love that God suggests. God says that love is patient and kind; it bears all things, believes all things, hopes all things, and endures all things (1 Corinthians 13: 4-8). Some of us are starving for love but we are grabbing junk versions of it to fill the void. When your body is hungry, it is seeking nutrients, not food. There is no such thing as junk food. There is just junk and food. Same thing for love. There is no such thing as toxic love; there is just toxicity, and there is love. When it is real, love will never fail. It won't leave you guessing, unsure, uncertain, or isolated. My single friends, even while you're starving for love, don't grab junk food thinking it will satisfy you. It will only make you hungrier. That's what I realized before I started fasting every Monday. The more junk I grabbed, the hungrier I got. So, I needed a reset. It's time for some of us to have a heart reset. What does that look like? It starts with identifying your triggers. What are the things that shine light on your hunger for a relationship and make you feel tempted to reach for easy love? Your desire for a relationship is from God. The temptation to reach for it in places that are only going to leave you unsatisfied is not. Maybe it's romantic comedies, perhaps it's social media, or even that one coffee shop you go to where it seems everyone goes on a first date. Identify the things that cause you to want to reach for the junk love and refrain from them for a time. Maybe it's just a day in a week like my fasting. Perhaps it's a longer period of time while your heart resets, and you meditate on receiving love from the right places. All in all, there's no different versions of love. There's no such thing as toxic love; there's only *true* love. If it is anything else, it isn't love. Just like there's no such thing as junk food. There's only food. If it is anything else, it isn't food. So, when you're hungry for love make sure you are fueling your heart with the right ingredients.

JOT THIS DOWN

There is no such thing as toxic love and healthy love. There is only true love. Anything else isn't love.

Day 19

THE GIRL WHO LOVES TO BE IN CONTROL.

Malachi 3:6: For I the Lord do not change; therefore you, O children of Jacob, are not consumed.

Confession time. Well, I guess you could say this entire work is a confession, and this one may come as no surprise to you if you've read any of my other works. I am a control freak by nature. In fact, I coach others using "control the controllables" as a practice that they can use to help with their nervousness or anxiety. "Controlling what you can control" and "trusting the process" have become such a cliché thing to say in our society. There's probably more t-shirts with those quotes on them than there are shirts with John 3:16. That being said, I don't think I'm alone when I take comfort in knowing that there are some things I have absolute control over, or I think I do. For so long I thought

I controlled how I showed up to my job, but then I was reminded that it's only by the grace of God that I have a body that can move to my job without needing assistance. I considered my workouts to be something I had complete autonomy over until I got injured and realized that it's only by the gift from God that I have the ability to move my body in a certain way. Most of my life, I felt this responsibility to control my inputs in my relationships. I made sure I told my family I loved them whenever I could, organized dinners for friends to get together, and communicated with a trusted one when I needed to talk. Then I understood God was the one who gave me those relationships in the first place. It's like your birthday. We celebrate every birthday without even really realizing we are celebrating something *we had absolutely nothing to do with orchestrating.* In fact, your "birthday" is your biggest proof that we are not in control of anything that really happens in this life. There is no way for you to go back in time before you were born to ensure that the specific sperm and egg produced *you* on this very day and age in time or sent you to the family you come from. The things we pride ourselves in being in control of are still only there to the extent of God's grace that reaches out to us in those areas. Initially, this made me unsteady. The thought of not being in control freaked me out. Then I realized that is the best option. Why would we want to rely on something as finite as ourselves to run the entirety of our life? It's not possible for you to control the oxygen you breathe or the process by which it is consumed in your lungs so that you can work, move, speak, love, and act. Thank God. Isn't it such a gift that God trusts us to steward certain things in this life but not all things?. To think that this God that loves me so much and knit me from the inside out is also in control of the broader ecosystem of my life gives me reassurance that He, and He alone, knows when it is best for the right person to come into it. Sometimes, I play a game in my mind where I think about where I'm going to meet the right guy. Will it be at this conference? Maybe it'll be next week at the gym? I for sure didn't want to go to this dinner party but maybe the right guy will be there? It's exhausting. God is in control not because He doesn't like us or trust us with our lives, but because He doesn't want us to bear the burden of having to figure it all out. He's already got it. Our job is to take the gifts He's given and steward them as best as possible. Maybe you're like me and don't have a partner right now, but you have an amazing group of friends. Perhaps you're single, but you've got an awesome gym work ethic. You're probably not in a relationship, but you're in a season where work is your top focus. Focus on the gifts God trusted you with and nurture them. Let God do the rest. I promise it'll be a better end result than spending this time worrying about it.

JOT THIS DOWN

Let God do His job.

Day 20

THE GIRL WHO REFUSES TO LEARN ABOUT MONEY.

Proverbs 31: 16-18: She goes to inspect a field and buys it; with her earnings she plants a vineyard. She is energetic and strong, a hard worker. She makes sure her dealings are profitable; her lamp burns late into the night.

Of. I have a feeling this one may ruffle some feathers. I know, as a society, we have made much progress in encouraging women to be financially literate and understanding. Yet there are so many women out there who are waiting for a guy to come along to give them a sense of security that comes with a steady income. Listen, I get it. Corporate work is hard. Making money is hard. I also fully believe that making money is by no means the only way of contributing in a family. I wouldn't trade my life for that of a full-time mom or dad right now. Everything they do is so centered around the growth of their loved ones, and there isn't a paycheck attached. Now, what I've seen to be true is that God puts seeds in our hearts for certain reasons. There's a reason some women and men dream of being a full-time parent. There's meaning behind the fact that other men and women dream of having a full career while building a family or not wanting a family at all. There's no right or wrong. Just different. There's a difference between not feeling the call in your heart to work a job that is bringing in most of the money for your livelihood and not educating yourself about money. The U.S. Department of Education reported that approximately 30% American men have basic levels of financial literacy while only about 10% women show the same (Annuity.org). Maybe you're like me, and you've sold yourself the story that you're not a numbers person, so you don't need to know about money or finances, but let me ask you this. Just because you're not a dentist does it mean you don't brush your teeth? Just because you're not a doctor does it mean you don't take care of your health? Just because you're not a hair stylist does it mean you don't wash your hair at least once a week? You don't have to be a financial expert to have a pulse check on your money, which will be the money of your family one day. We see this written in Proverbs 31. King Lemuel wrote Proverbs 31, and it is suspected by literary historians that King Lemuel is King Solomon. Lemuel means "belonging to God" in Hebrew, so the advice he was writing down is suspected to be from his mother, Bathsheba. It talks about a noble, Godly woman. There's a part in this passage that we, as women, so often overlook. First, might I just point out that this woman was a worker. It states that "her husband is well known at the city gates, where he sits with the other civic leaders" (Proverbs 31: 23). So obviously this family was well off because her husband was spending his time sitting in front of the city instead of working in the fields somewhere. Meaning, that this woman didn't have to work, yet she did. She "makes belated linen garments and sashes to sell to the merchants" (Proverbs 31: 24). She was crafty. She knew how priceless working was. It wasn't the money she was after because obviously she had that. It was the fruit that came from the process of dedicating yourself to something that made you better. Now, this is the part I want to really hone in on: this woman knew about money. She knew how to invest, and she knew how to spend wisely for a future profit. The Bible tells us that she "goes to inspect a field and buys it; with her earnings she plants a vineyard. She is energetic and strong, a hard worker. She makes sure her dealings are profitable; her lamp burns late into the night" (Proverbs 31: 16-18). Let's point out a few words here: "inspects," "*her* earnings," "hard worker," and "profitable dealings." This woman knew how to handle money, and she found that way not because it was natural, but because she worked hard at it. So many of us count ourselves out of being profitable or successful because we "weren't born with the brain to do it," but that doesn't come from genetics; it comes from hard work. Regardless of whether it is your heart's desire to be a stay-at-home mom or a working mom, you need to have a pulse check on your finances. This woman was a full-time mom but still knew how to take what she did have, make a good investment, and multiply her fruit. My mother is a leader in the finance space and helps families going through divorces navigate large sums of money. She says what breaks her heart most is seeing the number of women who do not know how much money there even is, and what they are entitled to. My women, my dear friends, whether you want to make money or not make money, please have an understanding of money. Money isn't everything, but it is a necessity for life. It is a tool God gives us to help build the foundation we find in Him. Take upon the hard work of understanding your money. This time of singleness is the best time to soak in what you can. Start anywhere: read, listen, or watch videos. Dave Ramsey is a great place to start. Soak it all in. Do the hard work.

JOT THIS DOWN

The Proverbs 31 woman was resourceful, she took upon the hard work to understand her money.

Day 21

THE GIRL WHO DOESN'T KNOW HOW TO LOVE HERSELF.

(John 14:16-17): And I will ask the Father, and he will give you another advocate to help you and be with you forever— the Spirit of truth. The world cannot accept him, because it neither sees him nor knows him. But you know him, for he lives with you and will be in you.

The truth is that I could sit here and give you the advice that every single person seems to give someone who is not in a relationship. "Fall in love with yourself during this time!" Now, I'm not saying that's crappy advice. In fact, it's true that as a single person you will never have more time than you do right now to fall in love with yourself. You don't have a partner or kids driving you in any direction. That being said, before you can fall in love with yourself, you have to know how and why you should want to. Before Jesus left for the final time, He let them know that they wouldn't be alone because His Spirit would be in them (John 14:17). The reason falling in love with yourself is so important is because the Spirit of God lives in you. The more you fall in love with yourself, the more you are falling in love with the Creator that made you. The One whose spirit lives within you. But before you can fall in love with something, you must first learn about that thing; that's the answer to the big question, "How do I fall in love with myself?" It begins with learning about yourself. The beautiful thing about this season is that you have time to learn about yourself. While you're single you're not distracted by learning about someone else. You don't have to take notes on what your partner does or doesn't like, so one day you can get them the perfect gift or foods that they like. You don't have to prepare for how they respond to certain things, so you can handle particular conversations with their more predominant emotions. Nope, none of that! Instead, you can use that energy to learn about yourself. The things that make you happy. The news that breaks your heart. What it feels like to have your heart broken. How you cope with heartbreak and happiness. Moments where you find yourself feeling cocky, or your ego takes over. The triggers that generate anxiety in you. The parts of you that come to life when you're doing certain things. Places that bring you joy and make you feel safe. What you feel when you're around people that bring out the best in you and make you better. What you feel when you're around people that bring out the worst in you. What the "worst in you" even looks like. Most people never become fully aware of these things because they don't stay undistracted long enough to really sit on them. The past two years of being completely single have been tough at times, but I've never been so in tune with myself. There are parts of me I didn't even know existed in my heart and emotions I didn't know I could feel. That's the gift of singleness. An undistracted opportunity to learn about oneself. In the process of that learning, you connect with your origin. You realign with your Spirit. Ridding yourself of all toxicity and distraction in the process, you begin to unbecome everything you never were because you're learning all about who God initially created you to be. If the Creator of you is Love itself then the more you learn about yourself, the more you are connecting to Love. That is how you cultivate self-love. It isn't a whimsical concept that can be written after a hashtag for a post boost. It's something about the nature of who we always were. Loving yourself comes from learning about yourself. To learn about yourself requires space to absorb what God shows you in the process. That is where your singleness becomes such a gift. An undistracted devotion to falling back in love with what you always were, which is a being made in the image of Love itself.

JOT THIS DOWN

God made you in His image. He is Love itself. Since you were made in the image of Love, when you reconnect with yourself, you uncover that you always had self-love.

Day 22

THE GIRL WHO IS AFRAID TO BE VULNERABLE.

John 20:27: Put your finger here, and see my hands; and put out your hand, and place it in my side. Do not disbelieve, but believe.

It was sophomore year of high school, and I was on a mission trip in New Orleans with a group of students. The guy I was dating at the time happened to be on this trip too, and I was beyond excited. I mean who wouldn't be? It was a week away from school in a new city with my best friends and the guy I was head over heels in love with. Better yet, the one girl who always flirted with my boyfriend and gave me anxiety to no end wasn't on this trip. An entire week without having to worry about her was a treat. There was a moment on that trip when the guy and I were able to walk around a bit by ourselves, and we had a serious conversation. We were able to open up about the things we were struggling with and stuff that made us anxious. I remember God giving me that little inkling to open up about how the friendship he had with this girl who I didn't trust gave me a lot of anxiety. I suppressed that nudge to the best of my ability. I didn't want my boyfriend to think I was some crazy, jealous girlfriend. I wanted to be the "cool" and "relaxed" girl and not one who felt uneasy about him having close friendships with certain beautiful females. Eventually, I couldn't take it. He'd never seen me cry up until this point, and I broke down. I showed vulnerability. I revealed my biggest secret. I wasn't as easy going as I made it seem. Some things that he did hurt me, and they made me anxious in ways I couldn't run away from. I was expecting him to freak out or confirm my fear that he would think I was crazy. Instead, he sympathized with me. He told me that some of my male friendships made him uneasy too. When I was vulnerable, it gave him permission to be vulnerable too. That's the secret about vulnerability; it's contagious. What I've seen is that most people are too afraid of opening up in fear that the other person will judge them. In reality, what opening up does is cause the person you are inviting in to identify things in their own life that can relate to the vulnerability you shared. When you're vulnerable, you aren't being a martyr; you're being a model. You are setting an example that others feel comfortable following. Being single, it's easy to let your walls go up, and think that there will never be a time when you'll even want to be vulnerable again. Whether it is a romantic relationship or not, God gives us other people as safe places to share what's in our heart. When we do that, we become a safe place for that person to share what is in their heart as well. It takes the utmost strength to tell a person the things in your heart that you find embarrassing, harmful, painstakingly awkward, and imperfect. It's really easy to shove them all down in a box and pretend they don't exist. When the time comes for you to be vulnerable with someone again, remember that it is a privilege to have that opportunity. That in your willingness to be vulnerable, you are giving the other person permission to be vulnerable as well. Know that there is a time, a place, and a spiritual compulsion required before you open up to the right person. It is a good thing to offer up the things in your heart that you'd rather keep hidden. Jesus showed His scars because He wanted the disciples to know what He went through was real. He felt the pain. He felt the sting. He felt the shame. He felt the weight. He felt that blood. He felt hurt. He felt the rejection, and he wasn't hiding it. Once the wounds become scars, he didn't hide them because they pointed back to His heart. Showing His previous vulnerabilities to His disciples allowed His disciples to bring their full selves to Him. Bringing your vulnerabilities to light will only encourage another brave soul to do the same. Do not fear vulnerability, my beautiful friend. Fear never brings light into the parts of your heart that feel more comfortable in the dark.

JOT THIS DOWN

To voluntarily be vulnerable by offering up your true self is to give the other person permission to be vulnerable by offering up their true self too.

Day 23

THE GIRL WHO FEELS THE NEED TO COMPENSATE.

John 14:6: Jesus answered, "I am the way and the truth and the life. No one comes to the Father except through me.

Now that I've been single for a while, I've started feeling as if I don't have the "right" to be single. Let me explain. Yesterday was Valentine's Day and for the second year in a row I didn't have that "special someone" to celebrate with. Last year, my lack of a valentine coupled with my ex-boyfriend's love for his new valentine left me feeling a bit nauseated. Nauseated? Jealous? Hurting? Confused? All the sorts. It's as if Valentine's serves as the aging reminder of one's singleness. Almost like how a birthday tracks your age, Valentine's tracks the years since you've last had love to celebrate. Last year, as I was anticipating that nauseating feeling grounded in insecurity, I buried myself in work. You see, the first couple of months of being single after my last long-term relationship, I felt it was socially acceptable for me to be without a man. It's like I had a single pass. People understood I needed time to heal before diving into another relationship, and many of us can relate to this. However, as time passes, it's as if people don't seem to understand the appeal of simply being single to be single. In fact, the longer you stay single, people begin to believe there is a reason you are alone. And typically, it's not because you're so amazing, but because there must be something wrong with you. So, the story I've told myself in order to prevent that from happening is "I must take on the identity of a woman that is kicking-butt in her career." Why, you may ask? Because as a woman, it's more socially acceptable to be single if you're at least making a career out of your life. "Oh, it's because she's just focused on her career." It provides an explanation. This has led me to put so much pressure on myself professionally. I can't just write a book; I have to write a bestseller. I can't just hit quota; I have to be the #1 sales representative. I can't just do the presentation; I have to be the speaker selected as the best. Often, when we feel insecure in one area, we begin to compensate in other areas. In fact, this is biologically natural. When one area of your body doesn't feel right, other elements of your body begin to take on more weight naturally to alleviate the pressure of the unstable part. What often happens is that even though eventually the hurt body part heals, the other body parts can start tearing down. The same thing happens in our lives when we try to compensate for our worth in other areas. The world emphasizes the importance of marriage, family, and relationships for women so heavily. When we aren't "achieving" in those areas we feel this weight to make up for our worth by achieving in other areas, and it's causing us to injure ourselves in places that do not define our worth in the first place. Jesus tells us that He is the way. He is the only thing that can connect us back to our worth, which is only found in God. We're over here bending ourselves left, right, back, forth, and we're breaking because we weren't designed to bend in different directions to try and find our worth. We bend toward finding our worth in relationships, then we bend toward finding it in our careers, then our families, our education, and then we break. What we thought was the way to worth was actually a step off its path. Jesus is the only way. So, while you can make the intention of being the best girlfriend, career woman, boss, mom, wife, or teacher, know that your worth isn't found in those things. It's not in the labels that the world puts on you. It's found in the One who is the

Father. When we walk that path, we no longer find ourselves compensating for areas in our lives that the world might define as "lacking" because we know that in Christ we are never in lack.

> **JOT THIS DOWN**
>
> **We were never created to bend back and forth for our worth. Our worth is found in Christ.**

Day 24

THE GIRL FEELING STUCK.

John 14:29-31: And he said, come. And Peter went down from the boat, and walked upon the waters to come to Jesus. But when he saw the wind, he was afraid; and beginning to sink, he cried out, saying, Lord, save me. And immediately Jesus stretched forth his hand, and took hold of him, and saith unto him, O thou of little faith, wherefore didst thou doubt?

I don't do "stuck." My skin crawls at the thought of it. I joke to myself that it is just an extreme case of claustrophobia that expands to more personal areas than being in a close quartered room or elevator. What do I mean by stuck? To be in a job, relationship, or situation where you feel you literally can't escape from. I remember the first company I worked for. I hated it. At first, it was a dream, but all of a sudden that dream turned into a nightmare when I realized the sacrifice it required. But, I needed the money. After a conversation with my mom, I realized I'm not stuck. Here I am having all this anxiety because I felt like this company is the only place I can possibly work to make a livelihood for myself. There are options all around that I was neglecting to see because my perspective was so narrow. I think we have that same narrow perspective in relationships, and the timeline God provides for those relationships. Listen, I get it. If you picked up a Christian-based book on being single, my guess is that you're probably someone who talks to God on a regular basis. You've told Him that you're struggling with your singleness in some way. Knowing that, I make the assumption that maybe you're like me. Some days you fully surrender to this season of your life, and on other days, you want to scream because you don't understand why God made it happen for other people so quickly. It's almost as if we find ourselves questioning His presence the most in the middle of our journey. Not the beginning of your singleness because let's face it, you didn't come into this world seeking a romantic partner off the bat. Heck, it takes like an entire decade on average for the opposite sex to even start noticing each other in that way. So, it's not in the beginning where our frustration with our singleness lies. It's in the middle. Time has passed. Maybe you've healed from your last relationship, or you desire a relationship to exist that doesn't require healing from. You just want something, and yet, nothing. Crickets. Drought. Nada. It's easy to think in these moments, where you don't have the gift of hindsight or the foresight of what's to come, that God left you. I love the story of Jesus walking on water for this very reason. Jesus didn't meet the disciples once they got through the storm and went to the other side. He didn't prevent them from a journey across the lake that would put them in the middle of a storm. He met them in the middle of it. I think He did this for me and for you. To let us know that He loves us too much for us to think we have to get through this alone and after we do, He'll be on the other side waiting for us. We think that "once we have the boyfriend and the perfect marriage then I've earned a relationship with God." Nope. He loves us too much to hold us back from ever going into storms where our faith is tried, tested, and strengthened. God loves us so much He meets us in the middle of the storms that come our way. He walks out to us. On our way to meet Him, even when we fall, He reaches out for us. He doesn't just want us to see Him, He wants us to know He reaches for us. Just like how He reached for Peter in the water. I promise you will get through this middle season. I also promise you are not stuck. You are in the exact place God needs you to be in for you to see Him and Him to reach you. He's got you.

JOT THIS DOWN

God loves us too much to prevent the storms, and also too much to let us walk through them without Him.

THE GIRL READY TO GIVE UP.

---

2 Corinthians 12:10: For when I am weak, then I am strong.

There was a time in my life when I refused to give up on anything. The idea of letting go of a dream I once had or even something that someone requested of me, I couldn't bear. I thought myself to be a failure, so I kept refusing to give up on things that just weren't coming to pass in that season of my life. In high school, I wanted my previous boyfriend to come back to me during my senior year and say that he made a huge mistake breaking up with me earlier. I had this dream in my head of us being together, and to give up on that dream had more to do with me feeling like a failure than whether I actually wanted to be with him. Did I really believe it was going to happen? Maybe not, but part of me never let go. To let go and not have any hope was scarier than holding onto something that probably was never going to happen. Kind of like this dream I had of finding the "right guy" one day. The past year of dating has made that dream seem less and less desirable. It's still there, but my perspective has shifted. I came home from another date feeling discouraged. I sat down and began to say to God, "I'm not giving up, but I am giving it up to You." See, it's not a bad thing to pause and reevaluate. After something hasn't worked out in your own strength, at least for me, I leave it up to God. So, I give it up. I give this desire in my heart to Him. If this desire is from Him, and He wants me to partner with someone to better serve Him then He must make it happen. God's purpose serves all. So, yes, make the plans, do the thing, but remember even in the parts of our lives we keep so close to us, we are designed to release those up to God for the sake of His purpose. God is Sovereign over your plans. Maybe you're like me, and you're sitting here thinking to yourself, "Is it ever going to happen?" And for you, it may not be marriage right now. It could be that all your friends are getting boyfriends and you haven't yet. It may be that your entire family has a significant other to bring to Christmas dinner while, yet again, you're riding this one solo. Perhaps it's just that your best friend is spending all her time with her boyfriend, and you're thinking that if you got a boyfriend too, you all could go on double dates, and you'd see her more. After all that wanting, you're at a place where you feel like you've been hitting your head against a wall because nothing seems to click. Then you internalize it. Is something wrong with me? Is there a reason I can't click with any of these guys? I've been there. I've thought those thoughts. I've walked many times down those mental pathways. Honestly, there is no harder place to be, but in those moments, you realize that at the end of your striving, God's strength can come in. Giving up isn't the same as giving it up. Strength comes from giving up my wants, needs, and desires to God in such a way that I am aware He's got it, not me. This is not to say that you can't put yourself in positions of discomfort sometimes and go on the date you're scared to go on, but at the end of the day? You don't have to manipulate situations to try and force a timeline on your life that God ultimately defines.

JOT THIS DOWN

Giving up is not the same thing as giving it up. Giving it up simply means refusing to manipulate situations to accommodate your timeline and submitting to God's.

Day 26

THE GIRL IN A LONGING SEASON.

Mark 6:7-11: And he called the twelve and began to send them out two by two, and gave them authority over the unclean spirits. He charged them to take nothing for their journey except a staff—no bread, no bag, no money in their belts—but to wear sandals and not put on two tunics. And he said to them, "Whenever you enter a house, stay there until you depart from there. And if any place will not receive you and they will not listen to you, when you leave, shake off the dust that is on your feet as a testimony against them.

The other day, I wanted to punch a girl through the zoom screen. She was, yet again, picking on someone on my team. The person that day happened to be me. You know those kinds of people who seem to enjoy making other people feel small? That's the worst feeling. As if you are a tiny, little *mino* who is absolutely incompetent at doing anything close to the standard of all the other big fish in the pond. I felt that way yesterday, and it crushed me. I felt so much anger but more sadness. Her words belittling my ideas made my face get hot red, and I wanted to shrink so small and disappear from the room. I think the worst part about someone making you feel small is when you have an audience watching it happen. It's one thing to be belittled in private; it's another to have everyone's eyes on you. Coming home that day, I was bawling my eyes out. I prayed to God asking, "Why do you create people who make others feel so hurt, cheated, small, insignificant?" That's when it hit me. The reason I am so intentional about being kind to other people is because of moments like these. I feel the pain of someone treating me without kindness so deeply. My passion for lifting other people up is because I know what it's like to be surrounded by people who only want to see you fall. The feeling that comes after you've been on the receiving end of a bully's wrath stays with you. Even after ten years, you will still be able to recall how time stood still in that moment the hateful words came from your tormenter. What I realized though is those hard moments were the catalyst for our intention to never make someone feel the way that we did. Freedom comes in contrast. The contrast of how great the pain was that you experienced, and how you treat other people because of your desire to never impose that on someone else. The same application of contrast is true in other areas of life. You see, what most people don't understand about their desire to be with someone in their seasons of singleness is that God is creating contrast in those moments of longing but not receiving. One day, you will be in a marriage (God willing), having a moment where you want nothing more than to go back to your single days where all of your time and money revolved around only you. There were no clothes, shoes, razors, hairbrushes, combs, socks, or dirty laundry to pick up around your clean house other than the ones that you intentionally left out. Everything was as you wanted it. It's in those moments you'll think back to this pain you're currently walking through. The pain of being single and wanting a partner will remind you of the gift you have in your lifelong partner. We need the hard in order to appreciate the good. You need these moments of praying alone for your future partner, so when you do start living life with them, you appreciate having a prayer partner even in the seasons that you're frustrated with them. You can't really appreciate love until you've experienced hate. You can't really appreciate kindness until you've met a bully. In the Bible, Jesus sent out the disciples with nothing to lean on, and with the intention they needed to rely on other people. Telling them in advance there would be people who would invite them in and also people who would refuse to help them. Contrast. Wouldn't you know there were probably more people who closed their doors in the disciples' faces than those who invited them in. The contrast of finding a place of acceptance after being rejected for what could've been so many houses in a row would increase the gratitude of the disciples as they completed their missions. Contrast creates freedom because it gives us distinctions as to what to follow and what to "shake the dust off our feet" from. The longing for a relationship, at a time when God isn't providing one, will lead you to a path where you further appreciate your partner in the seasons where it would be easy to idolize your single season.

JOT THIS DOWN

God is grooming you in this season of longing to more deeply appreciate a relationship when it comes your way.

Day 27

THE GIRL WHO THINKS SHE'S IN A WAITING ROOM.

Exodus 4:2: Then the LORD said to him, "What is that in your hand?" "A staff," he replied.

Tick. Tock. Tick. Tock. The ticks and tocks from a clock are forever ruined by the app TikTok, in my humble opinion. Just as the background noise of TikTok seems to constantly penetrate our everyday life, the pressuring silence of a clock, reminding us of time slipping by, also penetrates our everyday life. I was 21 and had just gotten out of a long relationship. I thought that was the guy I was going to end up with. All of a sudden time seemed to stand still. Everything was taking so long and yet going by so quickly. When you're in a state of desperation, time begins to move in slow motion. At 21, I was terrified that I'd never find someone to love me again. I looked at my current state of singleness as a waiting room. Watching everyone else get called, and I'm still at my seat wondering if my appointment will ever come. A lot of us think like that. We look at these seasons of life where we don't have a significant other as a "waiting room season." One where our life hasn't really started yet because we're waiting for a guy or a girl to define our starting point. Especially in a world that idolizes relationships, marriage, weddings, Instagram posts of your partner, it's so easy to feel like you're on the outside looking in without any confirmation that you'll ever be able to participate in those things. It's hard. Trust me. I know. It's not just the relationship you want; it's the inclusion of a world that celebrates partnerships and significant others. In the Bible, Moses was afraid he wasn't good enough. He struggled with accepting the season of life he was in, and what God was calling him to do. There was no external evidence that Moses was capable of stepping into the things that God needed him to do; only a word from God. At one point Moses was vocalizing his fear to God. Instead of answering Moses's question, God answered it with another question. "What is in your hand?" (Exodus 4:2). See, God will listen to your fears and concerns around what you lack, but at the end of the day, He will point you back to what you have. He'll always bring you back to the things He placed in your hand to conquer whatever season He's asking you to walk through. You might say, "Annie, you don't understand. All my friends are getting married. What will people think about the fact that I am 35 and not even dating someone?" Look at what you do have. Look at what God put in your hand even if it's the ability to raise and praise Him. He will not call you to a season without supplying you with the tools you need to walk through it gracefully. This single season isn't a waiting room season. It's your life. Live it. Lean into it. Praise in it. Look at what God put in your hand for it.

JOT THIS DOWN

Look at your hands. What do you have right now you've been neglecting to see?

Day 28

THE GIRL WHO DOESN'T FEEL STRONG ENOUGH ALONE.

Isaiah 28-30: Do you not know? Have you not heard? The LORD is the everlasting God, the Creator of the ends of the earth. He will not grow tired or weary, and his understanding no one can fathom. He gives strength to the weary and increases the power of the weak.

There's a shakiness when it comes to stepping out in faith especially in a season that you don't necessarily feel ready for. While a part of me is fueled by the anticipation of what God is going to do next, the other, larger part of me, is absolutely terrified. It's as if the entire world has been set in motion toward a direction that I'm not familiar with; I can't tell which way is up, which way is down, and where I fit into everything. When your life doesn't look like how you thought it would, it can leave a similar feeling. I know that when I write these words and share my pain, you're thinking about yours. For some of you, that's braving the wilderness of leaving a relationship you thought would be yours forever. For others, that's facing the fire of someone else leaving the relationship you thought would be yours forever. There's also a group of people who are facing divorce, break up, leaving a friend group, or getting laid off from a job. Regardless, you don't get through this life without pain. You don't get to walk through this life unscathed. Pain touches us all. There have been so many times when I've been in my bedroom at night thinking, "I don't know if I can do this alone." When I say alone I mean without a partner. I can remember the first time I had a massive heartbreak in my family. It was just after a relationship had ended, and I was already heartbroken. Shocked. That's how I felt when I realized that maybe I can handle hard things without a romantic partner. You never really know what you're capable of until you're asked to be capable. In moments where everything feels like things are getting out of control, some of us cling on to our only sticks of certainty. Most women are taught that we get certainty from having a romantic partner. So, when you're left in a season of pain and don't have a partner to lean on, you can shock yourself when you actually begin to heal in a beautiful way. I know it's hard to be in a point of your life that you didn't expect to be in. It's often in the most unexpected places that God has the chance to reveal a part of Himself that we didn't see before. To show you His strength, He may rid your life of the predominant things you had been leaning on along the way. Even when you're physically alone, feeling lonelier than you've ever been, God is there. He's the fourth one in the fire. He's in it with you. Through this entire season, His hand is on your life reminding you that, in Him, you won't ever lack strength. Is it still going to be hard? Absolutely. But, my beautiful friend, you have an amazing capacity to do incredibly hard things. "Better for you" doesn't equate to "easy for you." In the moments when you question if your strength can get you through, tap into the One who told you from the beginning that He will provide you strength when you are weak. Are you single? Maybe. Alone? Forgotten? Forsaken? Never. (Hebrews 13:5).

JOT THIS DOWN

You have a phenomenal capacity to do incredibly difficult things. "Better for you" doesn't equate to "easy for you."

Day 29

THE GIRL WHO FEELS SHE HAS TO EARN LOVE.

Matthew 6:33: But seek first the kingdom of God and his righteousness, and all these things will be added to you.

It was about 2 hours a day, 6 days a week. The 7th day of the week I'd do about 1 hour, and that was my off day. Yes, this is the amount of time I did cardio in the hope of reducing weight. A part of me genuinely felt that the skinnier I became, the more attractive I was, and thus the more loveable I'd be. So, I trimmed the parts of myself I didn't think would be desirable, and in the process, shoving myself into a petite frame of a woman that was silently suffocating underneath. In my mind, no one would want to get to know the inside of me if they didn't like what they saw on the outside. Love was something to be earned, and only those that played the game were rewarded. Skinny was the game for me. Thin was the rule. Love was the prize. Extra points came from tan, toned, bubbly, sweet, funny, and charming. For a while, I was winning the game just as my competitive spirit set out to do. Eventually, the game started to consume me. I began asking myself, "Is it going to be like this forever?" because it didn't stop when a guy got interested in me. Oh no, because who knows that once you catch something, you have to keep it. What you fish with, you have to keep fishing with. If you fish with your body, you're going to catch bait that has an appetite only for the body. What I wish I could go back and tell my younger self is that love isn't something you earn with your external appearance. God chose you first. He is the embodiment of love itself. *Love chose you first.* So, you don't have to go out trying to earn what you already have been chosen for. You don't have to strive and be good enough for something you were made in the image of. When it comes to a significant other, yes, love will take time to cultivate. But it won't be something that you have to earn. Like a flower that grows slowly through watering, sunlight, and nourishment, a relationship will grow when fed with the proper elements and in the right environment. It isn't something that you have to earn through anything external. A flower doesn't earn sunlight; it receives it. The world tells us to earn, earn, and earn. But God tells us to receive, receive, and receive. When it comes to the kind of love that God intended for us to fill our lives with, it doesn't come from external earnings but an internal focus. Focusing on Him and letting everything else fall into place. It's a love that goes deeper than initial physical attraction or witty humor. It's a love that lasts because of its foundational pillars focused on God Himself in the framework.

JOT THIS DOWN

Love chose you first.

Day 30

THE GIRL WHO FEELS THE BEST IS BEHIND HER.

Ecclesiastes 3:1: For everything there is a season, and a time for every purpose under Heaven.

It doesn't happen right after the breakup, and it really doesn't happen that often for a while after. It's during the season when you've been alone long enough that you begin to question if the big Man upstairs even hears your prayers. That's when you begin to romanticize the past. You forget all the ways that the last person you dated wasn't right for you and only think about all the ways they were. The bad times are shoved into a blurry image to be drowned out by the good, and you can't remember why you broke up with them. Also, the fact that there are couples all around seeming to emphasize your lack of a relationship leaves a pit of nostalgia in your stomach so engulfing that all you want to do is sit inside for the rest of the day. The enemy can trick us into thinking that the best is behind us. It can make us feel as if we are no longer active participants in our life but victims that were left with no love, no companionship, and no desire. You begin to miss a relationship that wasn't even real to begin with. One that, through time, has been glossed over and leaves you feeling as if all the love you're ever going to experience in your life has already taken place. That no man is ever going to look at you that way again. That no person will ever pursue you, love you, want to get to know you, chase after you, fight for you, or fend for you ever again in your entire life. When I begin thinking this way, all I want to do is hide. The thought of never having love again is a sad thought, but I am reminded by a quieter truth that there are no absolutes in this life. We tend to generalize our current situation for the rest of our lives. If we're upset now, we think we're going to be upset forever. If we're single now, we think we're going to be single forever. If we're overwhelmed now, we think we're going to be overwhelmed forever. If we're hurting now, we think we're going to be hurting forever. God reminds us that He is the only constant in this life. In fact, everything on this earth has a season. There is a reason you were in that relationship at the exact time, place, and circumstance. There's purpose behind the person

God brought into your life in that moment, but it was for a season. Just as there is purpose now in your singleness, God is doing a work in you that you may not feel or see at the moment. It will serve its purpose in the season God allocated it for, but again, it is for a season. It isn't forever. Nothing is forever except for the love of God. So even in your closet-floor crying moments, He is still with you. Even as your tears blend with the water streaming in the shower, this hurting season will not last forever. Old or young. Sad or happy. Wise or foolish. Active or sedentary. God will use every season for a greater purpose. You will feel loved again. You will feel pursued again. You will have someone look at you that way again. While I can't guarantee it comes in the package you are looking for at this moment, I can guarantee you have a Savior who is fighting for you every single day. While you are praying for someone to fight for you, God is endlessly fighting for you. While you are waiting for someone to desire you, God's thoughts about you outnumber the grains of sand on the beach (Psalm 139:17-18). Everything you are looking for in someone is already in God. He loves you enough to give you that desire in your heart (or else He wouldn't have put it there). Nevertheless, that will also come in a specific season. This hurt won't last forever, and I promise you that the best is yet to come.

JOT THIS DOWN

While you are waiting for someone to desire you, God's thoughts about you outnumber the grains of sand on the beach (Psalm 139:17-18).

THE GIRL WHO FORGETS THAT IT TAKES GUTS TO DO WHAT SHE'S DOING.

Joshua 1:9: Be strong and courageous. Do not be afraid; do not be discouraged. For the Lord your God will be with you everywhere you go.

It takes guts. Sometimes, that is exactly all you need to hear. You look around at the masses settling down, getting married, finding "the one," and all of a sudden you forget that most people in that scenario are people who settled because they're afraid to walk this life alone. In case you haven't realized it already, the truth is that you can go to Vegas tonight, under just the right amount of influence, and probably find a husband. The reason you haven't already done that is because that's not what you want. We think all we want is a partner to go through life with, but what our souls are looking for is a qualified partner to go through life with. One that pushes, challenges, loves, and motivates us to be better than we would be alone. Unfortunately, that is really hard to find. That is why so many people settle for the first fish that takes the hook. Needless to say, it's not necessarily the act of waiting that is hard. It's the act of waiting without knowing how long you'll be waiting for. Right now, I'm 25. I've been on so many freaking dates this year, and nothing has clicked. For the past decade of my life, I could only run into relationships that ended up lasting years on end. But now? I can't even find a guy who I want to go out with on a second date. If someone told me I'd find the right person at 27, I'd probably end up cherishing these next few years. It would be a sigh of relief because I know I have a few more years of singleness, but there is an end date. *That* doesn't take courage. What takes courage is when you've got to wait and there isn't a defined timeline. Waiting for something you can only hope and pray for but not be certain of. So, in case no one has told you recently, what you're doing is hard. It takes guts. It takes courage. However, what other story on earth would you want to be told than the one of a brave girl who decided to put her faith in God instead of the world's timelines? Stay in it. Don't settle. Even in the moments all you want to do is run into the arms of literally anyone because you saw your ex move on before you, your best friend buying a house with her new hubby, or three Instagram pictures in a row of someone younger than you getting engaged. God tells Joshua before going into the land that Moses wasn't able to lead His people into. "Do not be afraid." Honestly, when I read that in the Bible, I'd get irritated for a while. How can you tell me not to be afraid? Do you see what I'm going through here? I can't handle this! That is when I realized that God doesn't tell me not to be afraid because of my capacity, but because He is with me always. It's not a potential He wants me to reach but a promise He is keeping. We don't have to be bigger, stronger, or braver. We just have to align our life with the ultimate Protector who promised to never leave us in whatever fight may come. So, whether you realize it or not, He is in it with you. Through your lonely nights, your closet crying moments, your bathroom-crying sprees at a party, your fear around never finding a person, or your pain of attending yet another wedding that isn't your own. Remember you have the God of Joshua echoing His promise to you. He will be with you everywhere you go.

JOT THIS DOWN

It isn't about being strong enough to "not fear anything" but being aware enough to surrender your fear to the One who said He will never leave you and has the strength to carry you through.

Day 32

THE GIRL TRYING TO RUSH THINGS.

Proverbs 19:2: Desire without knowledge is not good—how much more will hasty feet miss the way!

Go. Go. Go. Go. Go. That is what is going on in most of our brains. We want results, and we wanted them yesterday. I remember joking in my first corporate interview that while most people in this world are "aim, shoot, fire" kinds of people, I'm more like a "fire, shoot, re-aim" kind of girl. If anyone knows the yearning for quick results, it's this girl right here. I think one of the greatest gifts God gave me was my ability to not overthink things and just do it, but it can also get me into trouble. The kind of trouble that leads to nights with endless anxiety. I keep questioning why I haven't seen results already. Results in what you may ask? Body, work, relationships, friendships, purpose, money, and basically the things that keep all of us human beings up at night. There's a beautiful thing about wanting to dive in head first especially when it comes to relationships. That feeling when butterflies get in your stomach, and you can only think/talk/dream about that person you're interested in. Especially if you've been in a season of singleness, and it's been a while since you've found that click with someone. You know the click I'm talking about—the one in which you didn't get the "ick" over a dinner conversation but wanted to get to know more. Just like we do with so many other things that grab hold of our heart, we expect it all to come so quickly. We want the strong, sturdy, Christ centered relationship right then and there, but there is power in the courage to take things slow. The best things God gives us are the things that need time to simmer. Time is the keyword here. So, my fellow friends who are similar to me in that you're a "fire" kind of girl, understand that there's a time to move quickly but not everything will come quickly. The best meals God makes are the ones in which time is the main ingredient. When it comes to relationships, the same is true. It takes time to really get to know someone. It takes time for someone to really get to know you. In this season of dating, have the courage to take it slow. The true fruit of life comes when we invite our extraordinary God into our ordinary moments. We must refrain from the need for His gifts to be given to us right then and there. Instead, we must surrender to the truth that He is the ultimate gift, and we have the honor to have him in every single second. The courage to take things slow. The keyword here is courage because that is what it takes: courage. It takes heart. It takes boldness to say, "God, I trust you enough to take it slow with You," and, in the process, may we be so lucky to get a glimpse of what it means to have "fire" in the Spirit vs. "fire" in the flesh.

JOT THIS DOWN

God I trust you enough to avoid rushing this season faster than You need it to be.

Day 33

THE GIRL WHO FEELS UNLOVABLE.

---

1 Peter 2:9: You are one of God's chosen; you are part of a royal priesthood, a holy nation. You are God's special possession, loved by God.

You're going to go through seasons in life where you feel like crap. I promise. No one can escape the moments where insufficiency and insecurity knock on your doorstep and make themselves at home. I've had so many seasons of life where I have felt so incredibly bleh. You know that feeling in which you don't feel physically attractive, and it all of a sudden puts you in a horrible mood, so you don't feel emotionally attractive either? It's like your center of gravity is so far off from reality that you question yourself physically, emotionally, and mentally. I have gone through seasons where I've felt this with both with and without romantic partners in my life.

I can honestly tell you, it's harder without. Why is it harder without a boyfriend? Typically, a partner is there to reassure you the voices bringing you down in your mind are so far off. Something that helps me in times of "bleh" is reminding myself of the truth. Even though I don't feel "pursue-able," I am pursued (John 4:19). Even though I don't feel "cherish-able," I am cherished (John 3:1). Even though I don't feel "love-able," I am loved (Romans 8:39). Even though I don't feel beautiful," I was made in the image of Perfection itself (Eccelesiastes 3:11). The enemy's lies don't come in like blazing sirens, that would be too easily detected. Oftentimes, they come as a whisper. You ate a bit too much, the next day you're bloated, and the enemy comes in to tell you that you're disgusting. You had a big presentation at work that you bombed, and that night, the enemy whispers that no one will ever cherish you because you fell short. From my history of challenging relationships with food and exercise, I almost always ask the doctor to never tell me what I weigh when I go for my yearly check-ins because it's always a trigger for me. Today, I went to a new doctor, and I forgot to mention it. When they said my weight as they wrote it down, I felt a shudder in my spine. I haven't weighed that much in such a long time. All of a sudden, a weight I wasn't comfortable with went from, "I haven't weighed that much in a long time" to "I knew that back fat from my sports bra was poking out more than usual" to "who could ever fall in love with someone who looks like that?" to "I'm going to die alone" to "God, I'm done praying for my future husband because I know it's never going to happen" to "you know what? Being a dog mom wouldn't be so bad." All this happened in probably less than the duration of my doctor's visit. That's how the enemy does it. We hop from one thing to the next without recognizing the spiral of unworthiness. Pretty nice trick to play on the ones God calls his special possessions. Why? Well, if I were the enemy, and I knew that the one thing guaranteed over the life of the children of the One I was trying to target was the fact that they were unconditionally loved, I would make my strategy to get His kids to believe otherwise. You will have times when you question what you're doing, who you're in partnership with, what job you have, the looks of your body, which outfit to wear, whether or not you ate too much, but please, my friend, never question if you are loved and worthy of love. God loves you so much, He thought you were worth sending His only Son to die for.

JOT THIS DOWN

You will have times you question what you're doing, who you're in partnership with, what job you have, the looks of your body, which outfit to wear, whether or not you ate too much. But please, my friend, never question if you are loved and worthy of love.

Day 34

THE GIRL WHO IS AFRAID OF BREAKING.

John 16:33: I have told you these things, so that in me you may have peace. In this world you will have trouble. But take heart! I have overcome the world.

Heartbreak is a funny thing. It's the most painful thing you can possibly go through. In fact, science shows us from brain scans that the same areas of the brain that light up from physical pain also light up from emotional pains. Heartbreak can be such a brutal experience that your body registers it as a physical attack, which is where the term "heart*break*" comes from. We feel as if we are breaking. I say it's funny because while heartbreak is arguably one of the hardest things we go through as human beings, it is also the most freeing. It reminds you that you were never in control in the first place. I remember the first major heartbreak that I had. I was probably 6 or

7, and I found my guinea pig, Oreo, dead in its cage. I instantly dropped to my knees and started wailing. I had never experienced death before this! We had an entire funeral for him out back by my rose bush. I just remember feeling so helpless. Here I was with my heart in pieces looking at this thing I loved so much, and I could do nothing about it. Have you ever been there? Your heart was in a thousand pieces, and there was no way to "fix" anything? You just had to surrender to the pain. Maybe you had someone break up with you and you weren't ready for it. You loved that person so much, and you didn't see it coming. Regardless of how you felt, you couldn't change their mind. You were entirely helpless in doing anything about their decision to end it. No matter how painful heartbreak is, we need it in our lives. It reminds us that we aren't in control. It's easy to hide away and put ourselves in bubble wrap to prevent us from ever having our heart broken again, but I encourage you not to do that. Some of us refuse to date, marry, or see other people because our hearts were so broken the first time. I want to remind you that God didn't give you your heart, so you could put it on a shelf. He gave you your heart, so that it could have life, and life requires vulnerability. When I get to the end of my life, I want to have tales to tell of the ways I loved and lost. The scars I bore from times I let people in and had beautiful moments with them. What a sad life to get to the end only to have a heart with no stories to tell. I remember when my Gwenny passed away. At the funeral, before I got up to speak, I remember having to collect myself because I couldn't stop crying. My brother, Demetrius (Gwenny's son), came over to me before I went up and told me something that stuck with me. "Love is worth breaking over." In this world, Jesus tells us that we will have hard times we'll break over, but we can take heart because love overcame the world. Out of all the things to have a broken heart about (money, bills, traffic, jobs, apartments, houses, things, materials) love is really the only thing worth breaking our hearts over. So maybe instead of putting our energy in trying not to break, we focus more on what we allow ourselves to break over. If your heart is to break, make sure it is breaking over love.

JOT THIS DOWN

Love is worth breaking over.

Day 35

THE GIRL BREAKING UP WITH "WHAT SHE THOUGHT."

Revelation 22:13: I am the Alpha and the Omega, the first and the last, the beginning and the end.

It's not always easy to see someone else get the thing you have been praying for. Even when that person is someone you love dearly, seeing God bless them with the thing that you pray for every single night can leave a pit in your stomach. The worst is when people respond to the blessing they've received with a "God is so good!" You too have been praying for the same but have not received it yet. The intention behind it is genuine and quite appropriate because it's giving credit where credit is due. Yet for the person who hasn't received the gift of their prayers, it can make them feel as though God is only good to other people. That adds to the pancake layers of shame and guilt that perhaps she did something wrong to be undeserving of the thing she's been praying for. What I realized recently, going through that in my own life where people I love dearly have found the man of their dreams and are starting to settle down, is that heartbreak from the breakup of *what you thought* was going to be your story is just as real as heartbreak from an actual breakup. This week two of my dear friends got engaged to the love of their lives, and while I am so incredibly excited for them, I found myself also feeling so heartbroken. I went home sobbing thinking to myself, "I didn't think I'd be here. I am 25, unmarried, and watching other people live out a story I thought was going to be mine a while ago." I felt so much pain around how my reality has shaped up to be against the story I had in my head. Sometimes, the journeys we create for ourselves in our mind are just as powerful as the ones that exist in the real world. This is why when we face something that causes us to confront the gaping difference in both our minds and the real world, it's natural to experience heartbreak. You're not heartbroken from something that tangibly existed out in the open, but it existed powerfully in your heart. You really thought you'd be married by now. You truly believed you would find the person you'd say "I love you forever" to and mean it by this point. You never would've thought that you'd still be feeling a little sadness on Valentine's Day because you have no one to share it with. No part of your mind ever in a million years thought you'd have to get on a dating app for the chance of finding love. Part of you is so shocked that you're still having to give yourself the pep talk about why it's okay to still be single. I get it. I really do. Because I've been there. Heartbreak from breaking up with "what you thought" your story was going to be is real, and it's powerful. There is, however, a reason we go through it. There is a reason we aren't the author of our lives and God is. There is a point to the fact that God is the alpha and the omega. He has already been where you are. He has already been where He is taking you. For every brokenness, we have the option to break apart or break open. Let it break you open.

JOT THIS DOWN

For every brokenness, we have the option to break apart or break open.

Day 36

THE GIRL WHO WONDERS WHY GOD LET HER HEART BREAK.

Ezekiel 36:26: I will give you a new heart and put a new spirit in you; I will remove from you your heart of stone and give you a heart of flesh.

I've had five injuries this past year. All of them kept me from running. For a time in my life, I really felt that other than God and my family, running was my true love. It consumed me. I was obsessed. I wanted to do it not just every single day but every single moment of every single day. One morning, my alarm didn't go off before class, so I didn't get my run in before 8 a.m. So, what did I do? I skipped class to go run. Scouts honor, I'm not making this up. I am saying this to illustrate the fact that I was so in love with running that not being able to do it was devastating. Every single time I got injured, I wound up in the back of my closet screaming to God and asking why He let this happen. "Why couldn't I just have this one thing go right?" "Why did you have to take this from me?" "Why is it that people who don't even care about running have the ability to do it right now, and I love it so much but can't do it?" Yesterday, I ran the furthest I'd be able to go in almost a year due to other injuries. It ended with me crying. The appreciation that weld up in my heart was something that couldn't be matched. I was back with one of the loves of my life and healthier than ever. It was then that I realized the gift God has given me through my injuries over the years. I could've never been injured, but had I never been injured, I might've taken it for granted. With each injury, came a renewed appreciation for what my body can do when it is healthy. Through the pain of brokenness, my heart has remained grateful for the new depths of my heart reached from the breaking. Some of us look at all the heartbreak we've been through in our life and think, "Why did this have to happen?" Needless to say, if you're a human being *you are going to get hurt.* And honestly? Thank God we do. Our heartbreak keeps our hearts receptive to appreciation. Through each and every bruise, we are reminded of how precious love is when it comes. It puts a tattoo in our minds to never take it for granted. Without the pain, we forget to celebrate the wins. Without disabled moments, we begin to take for granted our abilities. God is using the heartbreak to do heart work. With each crack, comes a new depth of love you can experience. A mature heart that can be even more sensitive to the magic love brings. Your heartbreak is not wasted. In fact, it is necessary so you can experience love to its fullest.

JOT THIS DOWN

Through each and every bruise, we are reminded of how precious love is when it comes.

Day 37

THE GIRL MAD AT GOD.

Psalm 10:1-2: God, are you avoiding me? Where are you when I need you?

When I get mad, I get quiet. Not the kind of peaceful quiet where you're looking at something beautiful, and you simply have no words to say because you are in awe. Nope, this kind of quiet is more like the silence before a volcanic eruption, or a massive storm. You'll know when I'm mad because even though I've tried to work on it, I can't quite un-master the art of passive aggression. From years spent seeing all confrontations end in arguments, I seem to have made an unconscious pact with myself that I won't confront, but I will be passively aggressive toward the person I am mad at because, in my mind, that is just so much healthier. Obviously, this is something I'm working on. I think you'd be lying if you acted as if you didn't sometimes fall into this category. So, what happens when you're mad at God? Did you even know that you can be mad at God? Have you ever even thought about it? Truth be told, 99% of the population has never actually had an honest conversation with God. Why? Because we think we have to be on our best behavior for God. That even though He's the one that made us and our emotions, He can't handle us on our worst days. Somehow because He's God, we aren't allowed to show him the not-so-great emotions that come up when we get ticked off about something. What I've found in my journey with God is that my relationship with Him is just that—a relationship. You can't build an honest relationship with someone based on half versions of the truth. The truth is that you're going to get angry at times, and sometimes, that will be toward God. But guess what? God can handle your anger, and there should be no one else you first go to in that state other than God. For most of us, it's not only what has happened to us that causes pain, but the things we wanted to happen and didn't. You thought you'd be married by now. You thought you'd have kids by now. Heck, you thought you'd have at least your first kiss by now. Yet, all of those prayers seem to have fallen off God's radar while it seems He's so acutely aware of all your friends' prayers as they get engaged and married. It's tough, I get it. I've had my share of cries, shouting sessions, and disappointment. What I've learned is that by including God in those emotional waves, I'm able to process with Him. I know what it's like to want something that God hasn't given you yet, and watch everyone you know get the thing you've been praying for. It's so easy to feel like God has forgotten you. We are most vulnerable in those situations because the enemy wants you to think you are forgotten. Yet, in those moments, we need to cling the tightest to God. How do you do that truthfully in those hard times? You let Him in on your anger. You tell Him you're disappointed. Cue Him in on all the anger in your heart. By bringing Him in, you can give it to Him. Let Him carry the burden you were never designed to carry. God has a purpose for your life. This I can promise you: though you may feel forgotten, you are never forgotten. Though you feel small, you are not small. Though you feel like God doesn't hear you, God hears everything and loves you enough to answer in the right way at the right time. Bring Him into the conversation. Let Him in because He can handle it. I think one of the reasons I admire David so much in the Bible is because he was so brutally honest with God about his feelings. The man God called "a man after God's own heart" told God repeatedly just how upset, broken, scared, angry, and fearful he was. If David knew to bring God into those emotions, why don't we?

JOT THIS DOWN

You can't build an honest relationship with someone based on half versions of the truth.

Day 38

THE GIRL THAT ISN'T PRAYING ABOUT IT.

Matthew 6:6-8: But when you pray, go into your room, close the door and pray to your Father, who is unseen. Then your Father, who sees what is done in secret, will reward you. And when you pray, do not keep on babbling like pagans, for they think they will be heard because of their many words. Do not be like them, for your Father knows what you need before you ask him.

Someone asked me not too long ago, "If you were granted every single prayer you've been praying to God for the past year, how different would your life look right now?" That hit. I'll be honest with you, I never used to pray much. Now to give myself some credit, I always talk to God a lot in my mind, but I realized as I got older that I rarely had a conversation with God out loud. You see, a lot of us worry in our minds and call that prayer. Prayer is a conversation.

Prayer is a connection. Prayer is the gift God gave us to change our hearts from the inside out, so we have better discernment on what needs to take place. God doesn't need our prayers, but through Jesus, we have direct access to Him. Do you want me to prove it? Look at the scripture above (Matthew 6:8). Have you ever talked with someone who is telling you a story you already know in detail? It can be so painful. God doesn't look at it that way though. Even though He already knows what we are going to say and what we're thinking, He gave us the gift of prayer to process our perception of the situation or ask the Spirit. I think about how many times I prayed *out loud* to God about my future husband or significant other. Honestly, not many. Oh, don't look at me with that face. See, I worried and thought about it in my head a lot. I figured that God already knows what I'm thinking, so why bother to take the extra step and talk about it out loud? The reason you "bother" to do it is because it's a gift. It's a mind, body, and soul changer. It's the thing that changes your perception internally. Through prayer, our Spirit gathers more information on who's worth dating, the guy that we're meant to spend time on, the person we're supposed to trust intimately, and the path God wants us to walk once we do come together. Without that, there isn't filtration. Think of a water filter that hasn't been changed in a while.

It's not the water's fault that it's dirty, but the filter's. It is the same thing with our minds. When we don't pray, we aren't filtering the conversations, thoughts, urges, desires, and wants in the way God created us to filter. It makes our minds murky. That's when we start to settle, lower our standards, and go against what the Spirit in us is trying to guide us to do. I'll repeat what I opened with. If you were granted every single prayer you've been praying to God for the past year, how different would your life look right now? Be the girl that can confidently tell her future husband, "I prayed for you. You are the physical indication of God's work in my life."

JOT THIS DOWN

Be the girl that can confidently tell her future husband, "I prayed for you."

Day 39

THE GIRL WHO IS GETTING GOOD AT SHAPESHIFTING.

Romans 12:2: Do not be conformed to this age, but be transformed by the renewing of your mind, so that you may discern what is the good, pleasing, and perfect will of God.

Shame! It's the ultimate shape shifter. The minute someone knocks you square in the face with a comment that sends you spiraling, it can make you change yourself in ways you didn't know was possible. I went out on a date with a guy a few weeks ago. This was my first date with a guy in a long time and it went really well. I was like, "Okay! Maybe I can actually do this!" Only thing was that he never texted after. You could say I got ghosted. Obviously while I had a great time, there was something that wasn't clicking for him. I somewhat forgot about it until a little while later when I ran into a friend that knew him. We talked for a bit, and she let me know that he thought it was never going to work because of how early I like to get up in the morning. He is a big night owl who sleeps most the day. It's funny to think how such a small thing can blow up in one's mind as "I'm not good enough," but that is exactly what my mind did. Instead of thinking, "God really protected me on that one there we are so obviously not compatible," I instantly went into the mode of defense. "I don't get up that early." "I could absolutely change my schedule at times." "I'm not good enough." "I'm never going to find anyone that will be okay with my routine." Isn't it funny how our minds work? Shame tells us that same story. The one that says we aren't good enough, and we need to shape ourselves to fit what someone else wants us to be. After having *successfully* done that in many relationships, I can honestly tell you pretending to be what you think someone else wants out of you will only leave you broken. The truth always comes out. It's why so many relationships fail. People start out so infatuated with the other person that they start changing themselves to gain the approval of the other, but once they have it? They slowly revert back to their natural selves. What ends up happening is two people in a relationship asking, "Why can't it be like it used to be?" Even though how it "used to be" was two people acting as someone they aren't to gain the approval of the other. That is why it is so important not to give into the voice of shame that wants you to change yourself. There's a difference between compromising on things that aren't as big of a deal in order to make things work with another, and lowering your standards altogether. That's why I made it a point to identify values in my life that are non-negotiable. These are things like belief in God, respect for health, family-oriented, and kind-heartedness. Other than that, interests can be adjusted but not values. Shame will also tell you that it's okay to date someone who doesn't believe in God. The minute someone judges you for waiting to have sex until marriage or being too rigid in your routine of going to church, shame will make you think you need to change those things. Romans 12:2 reminds us to not let things outside of us cause conformity to this world. I take this as a reminder that by following Christ, we will be different. This means that many people will not be the right fit for you, and that's okay. What's important is to bring yourself back to God, identify your values based on Him, and not try to shift yourself into approval by everyone else. You will not be approved or liked by everyone, but then again neither was Jesus.

JOT THIS DOWN

By following Christ, we will be different. This means that many people will not be the right fit for you, and that's okay.

Day 40

THE GIRL THAT NEEDS A REMINDER.

Ecclesiastes 3:1: For everything there is a season, a time for every activity under heaven.

Every now and then, I still need to sit and remind myself that there is a reason behind this season. I have no doubt that you are in the same camp. In 2018, I wrote myself a letter anticipating the single moments of my life that would follow. There is nothing more powerful than hearing your own voice from years past to remind you who to look to in times of hardship. Telling you there is a time for each season (just as Eccelesiastes reminds us). To hear His voice through your former voice in each season is where the message can transcend through any anxiety you feel in the moment.

6/25/18

Annie,

Hey. I love you. I love your heart, your smile, the way you worry about making others happy, and also the way you sometimes say "screw it" and do what makes you happy. I love your fire and your drive. I am so proud of you girl. Right now, you're very much single. It's an amazing yet terrifying time. You feel like you have the world at your fingertips, yet all you can think about is romantic love. Let me tell you something Annie May, don't settle for anyone who sends you nice texts and flowers. Any boy can do that. Find the guy that will lead you to Christ. Put Christ before you. Find the guy that will fight for you because he sees your value. The one that not only supports you but lifts you higher than you could go alone. The one that inspires you. Not to say he has to be perfect. That doesn't exist, but find the guy that leads his imperfect life back to his Heavenly Father. He who loves you for all your imperfections and brings you back to Jesus. Annie girl, hear me, I know it's hard and the temptation to just succumb to any boy giving you sweet attention is easier to fall into than waiting it out, but stay strong in your faith. Become the person who you're looking for, is also looking for. Trust in God. Trust in your devotion to

Him in this season. Trust in His timing, and you can't mess up.

I love you.

Annie

> **JOT THIS DOWN**
>
> **Any season focused on God is not a wasted season.**

40 days later,

I HOPE YOU NEVER FORGET THAT THIS IS A GIFT.

---

1 Peter 1:16: Since it is written, "You shall be holy, for I am holy."

41% of women aged 18–29 are single (Pew Research). I used to look at that, read it as 59% women are in a relationship, and conclude I'm not good enough because I'm not part of the 59%. Not being in the majority made me feel like I was doing something wrong. Then it occurred to me that in every other area of my life, I look at being part of the group that's different from the mainstream as a good thing. In fact, growing up, I sought after ways to make myself different from what everyone else was doing. I enjoyed being set apart, and that's not something unique to me. God calls us to be set apart when He tells us we are holy. Holy means to be "set apart." Now I'm not giving you full permission to isolate yourself, but I am offering you a change in perspective about your singleness. Instead of looking at it as a time that makes you different from the majority, look at it as a time that makes you set apart. It's a gift that most women never get to have. One could look at that statistic and read, "I suck. There's something wrong with me. Obviously, I am less than other women because the majority of women have found love by now, and I haven't." Or you could read it as, "Wow, most women never get the gift of this time that God is giving me. Obviously, there's something He wants to do in my heart in a way that most people never get the chance to experience." Falling in love is beautiful, but romantic love isn't the only kind of love there is. There are so many more avenues of love out there: big, bright, beautiful types of love. Love with friends. Love with family. Love for your coworkers. Love for your Creator. Love for yourself. Romantic love is but a mere piece to a much larger pie.

Listen friend, I know it can be annoying when people (especially people in relationships) try to convince you to appreciate this season when all you want is a boyfriend, but listen to me. All my friends are married or engaged, and I 100% thought I'd be too by 25. Now I find myself single, alone, and finishing the last chapter at a cabin I rented in the North Georgia mountains unable to express the amount of peace, love, and light in my heart. Peace, love, and light that didn't stem from a romantic relationship. Yes, it is possible to use your single time and turn it into something beautiful. When I fall in love again, I want to be able to show that special guy all I did with my time. Especially, all the ways I got to know God more in this season. There is beauty in the gaps. There is opportunity in this space. There is a gift in this time, but it's going to all depend on how you appreciate it. So, love it well because you will never have it back.

I've been coining this phase of my life (AKA the phase where all my friends are starting to settle down but I feel like I'm just getting going) as my "falling in love with Annie Mayfield" season. How can I fall in love with parts of myself I didn't know existed while I get this precious time? Take it. Copy it. Insert your name where mine was above. This is your "falling in love with _______" season. Oh, what a joy and a gift that is.

God is not against you. He isn't holding love back from you because He doesn't want you to have marriage or because He loves you any less than all the girls on your Instagram feed. God loves you so much that He's giving you the gift of living a season where you get to know yourself before having to tie yourself to another. Think of all the beautiful inventions, ideas, travel experiences, books, speeches, podcasts, jobs, giggle fits, decorating parties, and memories that are going to come from this time. I used to harbor resentment around my situation, and now? I praise God for giving me the very circumstances I once thought made me less. I can't wait to see all you do with this season. Cheering you on always.

Xoxo

Annie May

THANK YOU

Thank You For Reading My Book!

I really appreciate all of your feedback, and I love hearing what you have to say.

I need your input to make the next version of this book and my future books even better.

Please leave me a helpful review on Amazon letting me know what you thought of the book.

Thank you so much!
Annie B. Mayfield